LIFECYCLING

イデーが訪ねる、眺めのいい住処

The Story of 16 Inspiring Homes

IDÉE

CONTENTS

INTRODUCTION

それぞれに、ストーリーのある暮らし

たくさんの「こと」や「もの」があふれる中で、
いま何を選び、何を大切にして過ごしていくべきか——。
イデーが手がけるWebマガジン "LIFECYCLING" は、
日々、愛情とこだわりを持って暮らす人々の住処を紹介する
ライフドキュメンタリーです。

インテリアはもちろんのこと、仕事や生活、生き方といった人生観まで
さまざまな切り口のインタビューと豊富なシーンをとらえたビジュアル。
そこから、見る人がより充実したライフスタイルを送ることが
できるようなヒントやアイデアを発信します。

暮らしにおける美意識やもの選びの審美眼を大切にしながら、
自分らしく生きる人々。
ページをめくるたびに、きっと創造的なインスピレーションを
得ることができるはずです。

"LIFECYCLING"

LIFECYCLING by IDÉE is a series of live documentaries showcasing the homes of people whose day-to-day lives reflect an affection and dedication to the things they hold most dear. Interviews that approach their subjects from a variety of angles combine with comprehensive, compelling visuals to offer ideas for viewers looking to design their own more fulfilling lifestyles. Guaranteed creative inspiration on every page.

http://www.ideelifecycling.com

CHAPTER ONE. LOS ANGELES

ラリー・シェーファー

Larry Schaffer

OK store Owner
Los Angeles, California

蔵書も多いシェーファーのリビングに最近加わったのは、『Tortoise』ショップオーナー・篠本拓宏さんデザインの本棚。
「棚の高さがきちんと空間の幾何学に伴っているけれど、シンドラー的なものとは全く違うところが気に入っている」

白い彫刻的な出で立ちが特徴の外観とは変わって、一歩室内へ足を踏み入れるとその静寂な空間に落ち着くという。玄関すぐ横のキッチンへの出入り口が隠し戸のようになっている空間処理も印象的。イサム・ノグチのAKARIにはスチールのフレームが入り、床から天井までの高さをフルに演出していた

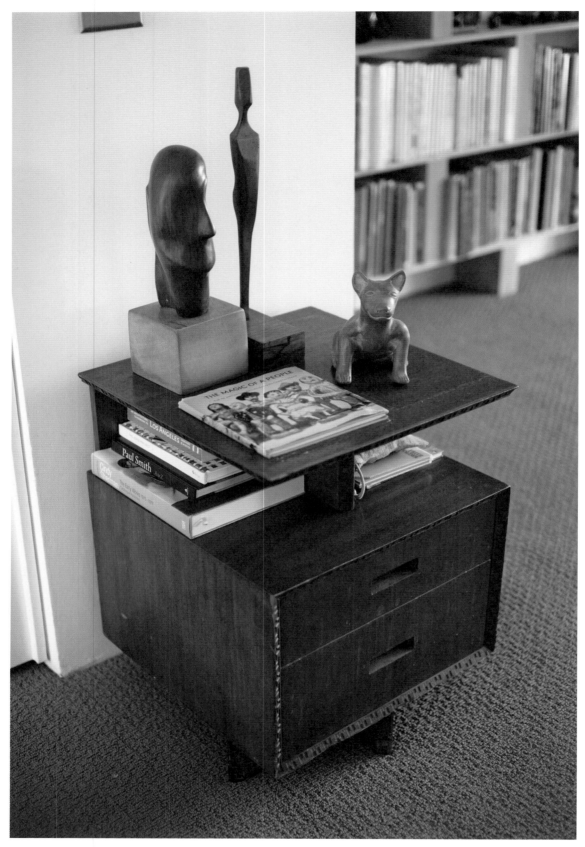

シェーファーの心に留まったものなら、北欧の陶器やガラス、日本の民藝ものから無名な彫刻オブジェまでジャンルにかかわらず棚に並ぶ

永遠にいいもの、残るもの、
永続性のあるものに囲まれて暮らしたい

「最初に記憶している建築物はフランク・ロイド・ライトのホリーホック・ハウスでした。当時14歳だった僕は『こんな風に暮らしたい！』と強く感じたのを覚えています」と、デザインショップ『OK store』オーナーのラリー・シェーファー。モダンデザインの歴史はもちろん、カリフォルニアの建築事情にも明るい彼は、2008年、1935年にR.M.シンドラーが建築したマクアルモン邸を購入した。その前に暮らしていたリチャード・ノイトラ建築の2階建てアパートについてはこう話す。「45平米と小さい物件でしたが、収納もたくさんあったし、すごく機能的な空間でした」。ノイトラよりも、よりアーティストで創造的だったというシンドラー。その建築もまた内部空間がすべてだという。「彼は依頼物件の丘に立ち、そこに暮らす依頼主のフィーリングを考えるような建築家でした。太陽の動き、風の流れ。多くの物件に建て込み家具をつくり、空間の幾何学を完璧に敷いたのです」。この家も、シンドラーの作り付け家具が空間のアクセントとなっているが、そこに置かれるオブジェたちの静かな物語は、よりシェーファーの個性を印象づける。

「『OK』の哲学には、これまでの生活が反映されているんです。僕が惹かれるのはどれも永続性を持つもの。今も使っているロイド・ライトの机とサイドテーブルは大学を出たての頃に買ったもの。当時その家具以外、アパートは空っぽでしたが、僕にとっては永遠にいいもの、残るものでなければ買う意味がなかったんです」。シェーファーは、最近同じシリーズのコーヒーテーブルを購入した。「できるだけ家と同年代の家具を探しているんです。でも、もちろん例外も。上司だったロイ・マクメイケンからの贈答品だったイームズ・チェアは、もう何年もともに暮らしている家具です。思い出の品である以外にも、僕はこのミッドセンチュリー時代のデザインに心地よい楽観主義を感じるんです。彼らの活躍した第二次世界大戦後は、戦争により生まれたテクノロジーを、今度は人々の生活を改善するために使おうという肯定的な流れがありました。そのフィーリングが建築やデザインをすごく面白いものにしていると思うんです」

そう語るシェーファーはまた、このシンドラー建築を当初の状態に近づけてリストアする、という使命を掲げている。「多くは増築されたり、改築されたりしたものがほとんどの中、このマクアルモン邸はオリジナルにとても近い状態でした」。一日を通して自然光が表情を変える室内の壁の白を、友人のカラーコンサルタントを雇いながら指定しているという徹底ぶりだ。「10年がかりのプロジェクトだと思って取り組んでいます。この家に暮らし始めて4年目。やっと庭のことを考えられるようになったところなんです」

プライベートでは、もっぱらコーヒーとカクテル担当のシェーファーだが、パートナーのマグダレナはアリス・ウォータースやヨータム・オットレンギなどの料理人を崇拝する、料理愛好家だ。「私の料理はロサンゼルスでそのとき手に入る旬の素材を、いかに美味しく調理できるかというもの。毎週日曜日にはハリウッドのファーマーズマーケットの行きつけの農家で買い物をするのを、楽しんでいます」。2人の休日は、テラスで食べるランチから始まることが多いという。また、よく夕食を食べるというテーブルは、彼方にアンジェルス・ナショナル・フォーレスト山脈を望み、とても抜けがいい。窓使いや天窓の配置でインドア・アウトドア空間を馴染ませてしまう、シンドラーの空間の妙がここにも生きている。「モダン建築に惹かれるのは何よりもその機能性です。最終的には建築家が暮らしの背景に隠れてしまうような物件が優れたものだと思っています。そういう空間に足を踏み入れると、単純に心地いいと思うんです」

最近、叔母の絵画を2枚飾ったというシェーファー。「アマチュア画家だった叔母は50年代にピエロの絵を、70年代にはこの抽象画を描きました。同一人物の20年を経ての作品という点も気に入っていますし、何よりも子供の頃のなじみの絵なんです」。モダンとパーソナルをうまく共存させる彼の生活は、整然としながらも、とても温かいものに感じられた。

Seeking out things with permanence, and living with design that has optimism.

"The first piece of architecture that I visited was Frank Lloyd Wright's Hollyhock House in Los Angeles, and I remember thinking 'I want to live like this!' I was 14 years old then" says design store owner Larry Schaffer who bought the R.M. Schindler's McAlmon House in 2008. "I lived in Richard Neutra duplex until then. His space was practical and controlling. It was very small but had lots of storage, and everything worked perfectly. Schindler is more the artist, exuberant and creative. I feel that his architecture is about plains and the space. He was the type of architect to stand on the hill and study what the sun is doing, how the wind travels. He had a very precise idea of where everything should be, so he designed the furniture to be built into the house, letting them define the geometry."

"A big part of my store's philosophy comes from the way I lived my whole adult life. I am interested in things that have permanence." For example, Schaffer bought Frank Lloyd Wright furniture when he got out of college, with an idea to buy something that would last. His apartment was empty then otherwise, but the same furniture is still in use today. "I love Eames and their generation of designers too because their work had optimism all the way through. The revolving idea that the designers can make people's lives better through application of technology was really exciting."

Schaffer is also dedicated to restoring the house to it's original state. "While many Schindler houses are altered, I felt that this one was already so close. We are thinking of it as a 10 year project. We are just getting ready to work on the garden."

While Schaffer prides in making coffee and cocktails, his partner Magdalena Sikorska keeps exhausting notes in her favorite recipe books. "What I cook celebrates what is available at the market in Los Angeles currently. We go to the Hollywood Farmers Market every Sunday, and I have my favorite vendors to go to. I'm inspired by the likes of Alice Waters and Yotum Ottolenghi, and their cue to cook seasonally." When they have time to spend at home together, they often have an outdoor lunch. They also have a dining table that looks over to Angeles National Forest Mountain ranges and Sikorska uses a bedroom desk that looks out the same. By ways of Schindler's details such as horizontal open or skylight in certain rooms, they enjoy the indoor outdoor border blurring.

"I love modern architecture first and foremost for its functionality, and second for its optimism that is exuberant. And I want the architect to disappear into the background. Same as what was happening in the design world, an idea to make people's lives better through architecture was there. And when you go to those houses like Neutra's and Schindler's, it simply feels great to be in them." While being the connoisseur of modernist design, Schaffer's recent addition to the house was his aunt's paintings. "My aunt was an amateur painter and in the 50's, she painted that clown, and in the 70's, she painted this other abstract image. I love that both are by the same person, maybe 20 years apart, and these are also paintings I grew up with." That fine balance of the personal and the universal, seems indeed the essence of Schaffer's life.

ラリー・シェーファー   *Larry Schaffer*

ロサンゼルスの南の郊外で育ったラリー・シェーファーは、子供の頃にフランク・ロイド・ライトの建築に遭遇したことからデザインに目覚め、1995年にロサンゼルスに『OK store』というデザインセレクトショップをオープン。ファインクラフトからプロダクトまで、悠久性のあるデザインを精鋭な目で選び、店頭に並べる。2008年にR.M.シンドラーのマクアルモン邸を購入。ロサンゼルスの建築事情にも明るい。

Growing up in California, Schaffer opened an interior design store in Los Angeles called "OK" in 1995. Since then, working closely with artisans and designers, Schaffer showcases various genres of products and crafts.

http://okthestore.com

02 / ヘザー・レヴィーン
Heather Levine

Ceramic Artist
Los Angeles, California

作品作りのインスピレーションソースは流木や木の枝、アーティチョークの花や珊瑚といったナチュラルなマテリアル

ダイニングテーブルの上のランプは、友人が手がけたもの。カスタム仕様の棚とデスクは
アーティストで木工作家のデューイー・アンブロシーノに作ってもらった

自分で作ったお皿に庭から採ってきたばかりのフルーツを乗せて。料理が好きなレヴィーンは、友人たちを呼んでおもてなしすることも多い

シルバーレイクの閑静な町並みに佇む住宅で暮らし始めて3年目。愛犬ピエールと自宅で過ごす時間は、日々忙しいレヴィーンにとって至福のとき。アーティストや職人の友人たちによる手作りの品々に囲まれた空間には、午後の優しい光が注ぎ込む

流木、果実、自然の作り出すオブジェや
人の手のぬくもりが感じられるものに惹かれる

「16歳の頃に最初に触れて以来、私は粘土に夢中になってしまったんです」と話す陶芸作家のヘザー・レヴィーン。2010年に暮らし始めた彼女の家は、ロサンゼルスの東側、シルバーレイク地区の閑静な住宅街にある。今現在も写真プロデューサーとして活躍する一方、ここ数年レヴィーンの陶器の人気が急上昇し、注文に追いつくのがやっとだという。つい最近、アトウォータービレッジの大きな工房に拠点を移し、今後は自分でガス窯に火入れする。「陶芸だと際限なくアイデアが浮かんでくるんです。自分のメディアを見つけた、と感じました」と当時の目覚めを振り返る。「特に今は、他にもカップやボウルなどの実用性のはっきりした美しい器の作り手が沢山います。私はあえてちょっと変わったものを作りたいと思っているんです」

今ひっきりなしに注文が入るのは、陶器の吊るしランプとウォールハンギングという壁掛けオブジェだそう。「吊るしランプを作り始めてもう6年になりますが、陶器特有の手作り感と貴重すぎない感じが好きです。シンプルな形に光が合わさることで、壁に別の世界が展開されるんです。丸い型抜きのランプはまるでディスコボールのような面持ちになって、陶器とモダンな型の組み合わせで部屋にまた新しいフィーリングを演出してくれますよ」。その型抜きされた粘土は、あてもなく工房にしばらく取っておかれていたという。「捨てたくはないけれど、素材として再精製するわけでもない。どうしたらいいかわからないまま、ある日、窯で焼いてみたんです。ウォールハンギングはそんな風に生まれました。いい使い道が見つかってよかった(笑)」

レヴィーンのウォールハンギングは、プロダクトながらどれもが一点もの。自分の手元にあるパーツを眺めて、それがどうやって一つのウォールハンギングになるかな、と考えるところに醍醐味があるという。作ってはバラバラにして、何度も組み直して、最終的にいいバランスになるまで作り続ける。「ウォールハンギングの魅力は壁にかかったときのデ

ザイン的バランスがすべて。一番初めに作った小さなウォールハンギングがまだ庭にかかっているんですよ。随分と長持ちでしょう?」

家の表と裏にそれぞれ小さな庭があり、野菜や観葉植物を育てているレヴィーン。「この前に暮らしていたアパートには全く庭いじりする場所がなかったので、とても嬉しい変化でした。そうですね、自然の作り出すオブジェに惹かれることが多いかもしれません。流木、マグノリアの実、それから育ち過ぎてうっかり花開いてしまったアーティチョークもここに(笑)。しばらく出張に行っている間に食べそびれてしまっただけなんですけど。それから手作りのもの、とくに"人の手"が感じられるものが好きですね」。その言葉を証明するように、彼女の家を見回すと家具やインテリア、それから壁にかかるアート作品に至るまで、人の手のぬくもりが感じられるものがたくさんあることに気づく。「ここにあるもののほとんどは友人の作ったものばかりなんです」。ダイニングテーブルの上にかかるランプ、カスタムの机と棚、そして小さなスツールが集まったテーブルはすべて友人たちの手作りのものだという。「小さなスペースに暮らしているので大きな家具を入れたくなかったんです。とくにモジュラー式に形の変えられるコーヒーテーブルはぴったりでした」

休みの日には家での時間を思う存分楽しむという。「料理が好きなので、何かを作って友人たちを招いたりもします。多くの人にとって食は社交の大切な要素だと思います。特に食の面で今ロサンゼルスはいろんな新しい動きがおきていますから」。1994年にニューヨークから西海岸に移り住んだ母親を訪ねてアメリカ横断してきたレヴィーンは、戻ることなくここでの生活を始めたという。「仕事や旅でさまざまな場所を訪ねるのはもちろん大好きです。でも家に帰ってくることも大好き。自分の選んだ街で生活を築き上げたら、それを後にするのはなかなか難しいですよね。もちろん不服だったら別ですが、私はここでの生活が大好きなんです」

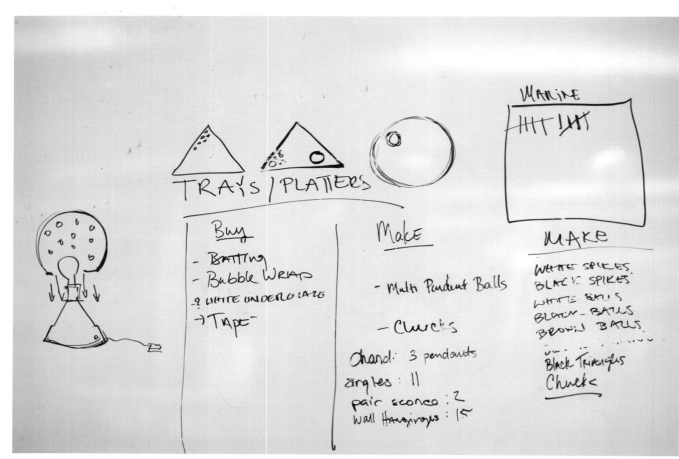

TRAYS / PLATTERS

Buy
- BATTING
- BUBBLE WRAP
- 2 WHITE UNDERGLAZE
- → TAPE

Make
- Multi Pendant Balls
- Chucks

chand: 3 pendants
singles: 11
pair sconce: 2
Wall Hangings: 15

MARINE
HHT | HHT

MAKE
WHITE SPIKES
BLACK SPIKES
WHITE BALLS
BLACK BALLS
BROWN BALLS.
Black Triangles
Chucks

I like things hand made, things that feel a little touched by human.

"I first worked with clay when I was 16, and ever since then, it was somewhat of an addiction" confesses Heather Levine in her quaint home in Los Angeles. She bought this house in 2010, and has just moved into her new studio in Atwater Village. Still keeping herself at it with photo production work, Levine has been the busiest in the last couple of years with her ceramic endeavor. "With clay, it was a never ending flow of ideas. I felt that I found my medium," says Levine about her early revelation. "I like making an object that is not so obviously utilitarian. I feel that especially now there are so many people making beautiful cups and bowls. For me, it would have to be something that is a little unique."

Her clay lamps and wall hangings are the things that are keeping her busy. "I have been making the hanging lamps for about 6 years. I like it to feel hand made, but I do try and not make anything too precious. I'm interested in the simple shapes and what the light does with them in relation to the walls. Circles will make disco ball effects almost, and there are certain shapes I am drawn to. The combination of clay and modern shapes are attractive because they communicate a different feeling in the room." Those simple shapes that were cut out from the lamps apparently sat around in her studio for a long time. One day Levine decided to fire them, and the wall hanging was born. "I didn't want to throw away all that clay, and I was hoarding all these parts. I'm glad I found good things to do with them."

Levine's wall hangings are all one of a kind. She will sit for hours in the end reworking the balance of all of the elements multiple times. "The balancing act is really appealing, I still have my first wall hanging in my yard - same strings and all, just those two tiny pieces."

Levine's house now has a front and back garden, where she grows vegetables and plants. "I moved from a place that had no garden space so I was really excited. I tend to collect natural objects like drift wood, Magnolia pods, and even the accidentally flowered artichoke! I was traveling for work, and missed a chance to eat them in time. I also like things hand made, things that feel a little touched by human." To prove her words, her living room is filled with beautifully handcrafted interior items, or original art. "Most of the things in my house are things that my friends made. Dining table lamp is by Dan Knapp, and Dewey Ambrosino made the desk and those stools that are my coffee table. I live in a little space, and did not want to crowd it with large furniture, so it was perfect."

On her day off, which is seemingly rare to come by these days, Levine indulges in time at her home, intentionally not making plans. "I love to cook, and will gather around food with friends. I think for many people, food is their social activity, and there are so many exciting things happening in Los Angeles right now." The transplant from New York City has made a cross country trip in 1994 and never left. "I love visiting so many places, through work and travels, but I also like coming home. You build a life in the city, and it's hard to leave behind. Unless you are unhappy, but I'm happy here!"

ヘザー・レヴィーン　*Heather Levine*

ニューヨークのど真ん中、マンハッタンで生まれ育ったレヴィーンは、1994年以来ロサンゼルスを拠点に生活している。一点ものとプロダクトの狭間の面白さを強みとし、吊るしランプやウォールハンギングなど、近年人気を博している。移転したばかりの大きな工房にはガス窯があり、今後は他の陶芸作家の作品も焼けるようにする予定だという。

Born and raised in New York City, Levine now calls Los Angeles her home. Her ceramic works have unique character, which often strike a balance between one of a kind object and well made product. Recently relocating her studio to a bigger space with a gas kiln, Levine is also planning to invite other ceramic workers to fire there.

http://www.heatherlevine.com

03/

クリス・ジョハンソン　ジョハンナ・ジャクソン
Chris Johanson, Johanna Jackson

Artists
Los Angeles, California

家中にある、キルトブランケットやダイニングチェアの布張りも含め、布ものはすべてジャクソンが手がけた。
木工家具は道端で見つけてきた素材でジョハンソンが作ったものだという

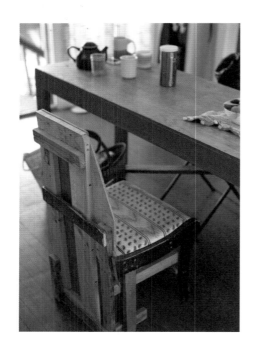

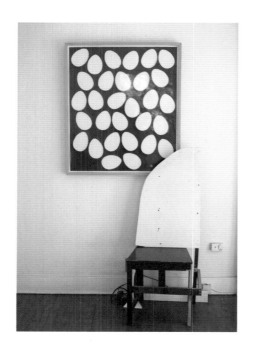

必要なものだけをできるだけ自分たちで作り、無駄なものは一切持ち込まない、日常空間自体がアート作品のような
2人のロサンゼルス暮らし。彼らが作る椅子やテーブルは、既製品にはないオリジナリティあふれるものばかり

元々、ウォルト・ディズニー・カンパニーの職員のために造られた集合住宅であったという建物は、車通りの頻繁な通りから階段を
50段ほど上った場所にある。傾斜と木々によって形作られる、静かなツリーハウスのような佇まいが印象的。ジョハンソンは今一
番お気に入りのピーター・シャイアーのマグを「世界一良くデザインされたオブジェ」と豪語する。一方ジャクソンは、自分でテキス
タイルをデザインするほど布にこだわる。「今度は自分で布にプリントしてみるつもり」と、さらに手仕事の可能性を追求する

道端に落ちていたクレートが椅子に。
いい長さの板を見つけたら家具作りが始まる

「ロサンゼルスでの庭いじりは水がすべてなんだと気づきました。水を撒いただけであちこちからいろんな植物が芽を出してきて」と話してくれるのはジョハンナ・ジャクソン。夫のクリス・ジョハンソンと暮らす家は、道路から真っすぐに階段を上がりきった傾斜の一番上に位置している。木陰がたくさんある庭では愛犬レーズンも涼しそうにしている。「秘密の場所なんですよ、ここは」とうそぶくジョハンソンは先ほどキッチンで調理してきた料理の解説をしてくれる。「人参、イモ、ハラペーニョとトルティーヤ、それに卵を加えてランチェロソース（メキシコ式トマトチリソース）をかけただけ。僕はどちらかというとグルービーな料理人ですが、ジョハンナはかなり本格的」。そのジャクソンは最近夢中になっているというカヴァスという飲み物の話をする。「発酵させたビーツで、そのまま冷やして飲んだりソーダ水で割ったり。美味しいんですよ」

出会いの地、サンフランシスコを2002年に離れ、オレゴン州のポートランドに移住し、ここ2年はポートランドとロサンゼルスを行き来している2人。「気候が暖かくて太陽がしっかり射す土地では、体も心もリラックスして、幸せの疑似状態になると思うんです。時間の感覚が緩くなるのもいいですね。あれは先週だっけ、それとも先月？ てな具合にね」とジョハンソン。「それから社会的多様性もすごく楽しいです。小さな職業大学のピクルス教室を受講したら、自前のメイソンジャーを持ってきたのは私だけ。メイソンジャーのデザインを褒められたりして、正直ビックリしましたけど、すごく新鮮でした」とジャクソンは言う。「アートの世界のテンションとは真逆ですね」と足すのはジョハンソン。ロサンゼルスの家は、ものと作品に埋め尽くされているというポートランドの家とは違って、ミニマルの極み。「いらない物は一切持ち込まない、買わない、というのがルールです」。見回してみるとほとんどが2人による手作り、ないしは友人アーティストの作品だということに気づく。「持ってきたのは洋服少しと工具のみ。ほとんどの家具はタダで手に入った

材料で作ったんです。道端に落ちていたクレートが椅子になったり、いい長さの板が落ちていたら、『あれ、これダイニングテーブルにちょうどいいかも』となったりして、そんな具合に家具作りが始まるんです」とジョハンソン。つい先日キッチンの鍋掛けも作ったのだという。

数年前にジャクソンは、絵画からより実用価値のある布や毛糸を通しての手仕事の表現にシフトしている。「糸の感触が好きですし、人間と繊維の関係性にもとても興味があります」。そう話すジャクソンのアートはテキスタイルデザインやキルトの形で楽しむことができる。「僕らは成長しながら新しいことに挑戦したいと思っています。だから家具を作り始めたんです。マインドを使ってもっといろんなことがアートとしてできるはず。人生自体が作品のはずで、作品が人生ではない。自分の時間を持たないと、言いたいこともなくなっちゃうんじゃないかな」とジョハンソンが言い添える。

ニューヨークのザ・スタンダードホテルの噴水彫刻に取り組んでいるという2人のスタジオには、抽象的な物から実体的なモチーフまで、さまざまな形の陶器オブジェが焼き上がっていた。「針金やセメントで継ぎ合わせるので、割れていたって大成功。窯を借りている近くの陶芸工房の人たちはヒビや壊れがあると、可哀想な顔をして見ていますが、僕らにしてみれば『やった』という感じ」。どんな結果でも大歓迎な様子はジョハンソンの一人芝居に見て取れる。「へんてこなのができてきたね。『僕はリラックスした、ただの形容詞的なものです。銃なんかではありません』何を窯に入れたかも忘れちゃっているから面白いね」。そんな自由な発想が、彼らのエネルギーそのものとして作品に、常に反映されていく。

「もっとノマド的でいいと思っています、今は。場所やものへの執着を削いだところを目指しています」。2人のストイックな暮らしに誰しも感銘を受けることは間違いない。同時に何でも手で作ることができるという可能性を持つ強みも考えさせてくれる。

Making furniture with found material, and how length of wood could define a dining table

"I see now in LA that if you water, then plants grow. I just watered over here and there, and these appeared!" says Johanna Jackson, sitting in the yard by the house she resides in with her husband Chris Johanson. This used to be a Disney Studio residence, and several units share the stairs up the hill from the street, with their place nestled at the very end. Johanson eventually appears from the kitchen with a plate full of hearty looking food. "I just grilled some carrots, potatoes, jalapeno peppers, tortillas, and put some egg and ranchero sauce. I'm the groovy cook, and Johanna's a serious cook. She really gets into stuff." And it's true, as Jackson talks about Kvass making that she's been into lately. "It's a fermented beet drink, you can drink it cold or with soda water. The culture is the whey, and it tastes really good."

After moving away from San Francisco in 2002, where the couple met, they set their base in Portland, Oregon while they traveled around a bunch. "It was a nice place to come back to for a while, and we wanted a house" remarks Jackson about their move. They now have been splitting their time between Portland and Los Angeles for about 2 years. "When the weather's hot and there's plenty of sun, you are relaxed and I think it's a form of happiness." And the social diversity has been exciting too, says Jackson, who found herself the only person to come in with a mason jar at a technical collage's pickling class. "Those environments are exciting for me," says Jackson.

They made a conscious change in what to bring into the house in Los Angeles. "Our rule was not to bring anything we didn't want, and not to buy anything. We didn't bring anything out here but our clothes and tools" says Johanson, "so everything that's in the house is made from materials found on the street, or got for free somewhere. For the dining table, I found a piece of wood, and thought oh, that's a good length for the table." And that's how everything seems to begin taking shape. "Chris made the most incredible pot racks recently. It totally opened up the kitchen, isn't it amazing?" "Love is in the air, obviously" shrugs Johanson.

Jackson moved away from traditional painting practice a couple years back, and now works heavily with her hands using utilitarian materials. "I like people expressing themselves. I like the feeling of the strings, and the relationship with the human and the fiber." Her drawings and ideas are seen around the house on fabrics making a quilt or a even a shower curtain. "And knitting, I love how I can do it anywhere. I've recently come across a Scottish knitting book, and saw a woman back in the day walking and knitting!" excitedly says Jackson. Johanson adds, "I've been making art since the 90's. I always think that art is about learning new things. We are just trying to grow, trying out new things. That's why we started making furniture and started moving away from just the traditional art form. There's got to be other things you can do with your mind. I mean, the piece is the life, and piece isn't always about the show. You got to have your down time so that you have some things to say."

クリス・ジョハンソン *Chris Johanson* ／ ジョハンナ・ジャクソン *Johanna Jackson*

ペインティング、彫刻、ビデオに音楽とマルチに活躍するクリス・ジョハンソンと、布や毛糸と併せてビデオ制作もするジョハンナ・ジャクソンのアーティスト夫婦は、近年コラボレーション作品を多く発表している。2012年にはUCLAハマー美術館が2人の家具をパーマネントコレクションとして購入し、現在も展示を続けている。

Both working in a wide variety of mediums, Johanson makes paintings, 3D sculptures as well as video and music, while Jackson's focus is with fabric, yarns, and sometimes video. They have worked on more collaborative pieces in the recent years, and in 2012, UCLA Hammer Museum purchased and showcases their couches, chairs, and tables as part of their permanent collection. They work out of a studio in Highland Park.

http://chrisjohanson.com   http://www.johannajackson.com

04 / 八木 保
Tamotsu Yagi

Art Director
Los Angeles, California

ジャン・プルーヴェのテーブルのある空間。シャルロット・ペリアンのテーブルとスツールには普段雑誌などを置く。
壁一面のマウロ・ジャコーニのドローイング作品が目を引く

一過性の性質を持つコンセプトアート作品から、木の実や種子、そして鳥の巣や卵まで、デザインのインスピレーションのもとは多岐にわたる

18 FUTURA BOLD

小学校の壁だったプルーヴェの建築パーツは2階オフィスのパーテーションに使われていた。世界に数脚しかないというカンガルー・チェアもオフィス家具としてしっかり役割を果たせば、希少なセルジュ・ムーユのオリジナル照明も活躍する。サイ・トゥオンブリーのリトグラフは貴重なインスピレーションソース

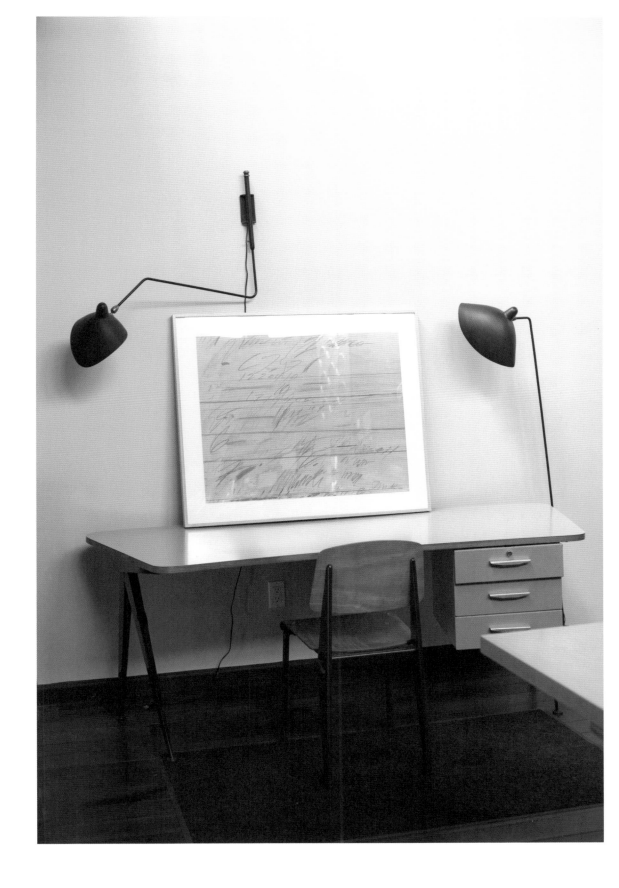

自然光が生活のメリハリを作る
住宅街のLIVE／WORKスペース

ロサンゼルスの西側にあるベニスビーチの、閑静な住宅街に住居兼仕事場となる空間を見つけたアートディレクターの八木保さん。長く暮らしたサンフランシスコを離れて、気候の良いロサンゼルスに移住してきたのは、仕事と暮らしの距離をもう少し近づけるためだったという。

「サンフランシスコで"LIVE／WORK"の物件を見つけようと思うと、インダストリアルな空間に行き着くことが多い中、ロサンゼルスにはこういった住宅街に交じり込んだ物件がたくさんあったんです」と3階建てのアトリエに招き入れてくれた八木さん。ジャン・プルーヴェやシャルロット・ペリアンの家具のコレクターとしても知られる彼は、それらの家具をただ集めるだけではなく、仕事場や生活の中で使うことを大切にしている様子が伝わってくる。この物件に決める時も、娘の理都子さんにすべての家具や建築パーツが入ることを確認してもらったのだという。

3階まで吹き抜けたメインの作業テーブルが置かれる空間と、1階にあるキッチンを隔てるのは、プルーヴェのコンゴのアパートの外装の一部である。時間帯によってきつく差し込む光を、このシャッターを自在に調整してうまく扱う。「『サン・シャッター』が見事にはまったのには驚きました。ここは、サンフランシスコと違って光がきついんです。本当はもっとアート作品を飾りたいのだけれど、退色を考えると控えざるを得なくて」。そう説明してくれる八木さんの背後には、風が入り込むとふわりと動く、大きなドローイング作品がインストールされている。これはアルゼンチンの作家、マウロ・ジャコーニの作品で、日焼けや風の動き、それから壁に付着しているテープのシミなども、すべて作品の一部と言うユニークなインスタレーションなのだそうだ。

八木さんのアトリエには、息子の巧さんや、プロジェクトベースで携わる理都子さんの他に、何人かのスタッフが常に出入りをしている。ロサンゼルスに拠点を移して3年がたった今、八木さんの言葉の端々に暮らしと仕事が密接に入り交じる様子が楽しげにうかがえる。「この辺りはランチ

を食べに行くにも、駐車の問題や移動距離など、作業を中断して行くには時間がかかり過ぎてしまう。だから僕らは1時間以内の料理、ということを条件に、よく交代でランチを作るんです。使ってみたらやはり住居兼用の物件なのでとてもキッチンが使いやすい。デザインは料理みたいなもので、下ごしらえをきちんとすることがレイアウトや文字決めといった細かな作業に似ていると思うんです。下ごしらえの上手な人は、デザインも上手なんじゃないかな？」と八木さん。案内されたキッチンを見回すと、キュウリはもとより、ソーセージや卵のピクルスの瓶、そして紅茶キノコの大瓶も目に入ってくる。「ピクルスの天ぷら、食べたことあります？ 美味しいですよ」と説明されれば、その味を楽しく想像してみる。それぞれのスタッフに得意料理があって、毎週金曜日に近くのファーマーズマーケットで買って来た旬の食材を、一週間のうち数回、皆で調理して食べる。フォー、麻婆豆腐、タイカレーやサバ塩など、下ごしらえさえきちんとすればさっと料理できるメニューが人気だとか。この日はスタッフの伊藤心介さんが、古道具のすり鉢で作るフレッシュペストパスタを作った。材料はごく簡単、ファーマーズマーケットで買ってきた旬のフレッシュバジル、ガーリック、パインナッツ、パルメザンチーズ、オリーブオイルに塩。風呂敷に包んで重ね置きをしていた大器のすり鉢は京都で見つけてきた古道具だそうで、精進料理のごま豆腐などを作る時に使われていたもの。それを使って伊藤さんが手際良く素材をすりあわせていく。白い器に鮮やかな緑のソースの絡まったパスタが映え、食事もお皿の上のデザインだな、と実感させてくれる。

もう一つロサンゼルスに拠点を移して変わったこと。仕事は自然光とともに、と決めているという。「24時間、同じ光ということがないので生活にメリハリができていいですよ。西日のきつくなる頃に、大概仕事を切り上げるようにしています」。光や食材を通して、ロサンゼルスにもしっかりと巡る季節を感じながら、丁寧に生活している様子が感じられた。

A good prepping job is equivalent to making good design decisions

Near Venice Beach on Abbot Kinney Boulevard, art director Tamotsu Yagi found a live/work space in a quaint residential neighborhood. His relocation from San Francisco to Los Angeles 3 years ago was also to bring the work component a little bit closer to life, explains Yagi.

"When you try to find a live/work in San Francisco, you often come across an industrial area with larger structures. But here in LA, there were many places like this that blend into the residential neighborhoods." His studio is 3 stories high, and pleasantly scattered with Jean Prouvé and Charlotte Perriand furnitures. In fact one will quickly learn that these rare pieces are the core of the function around the office. Upon signing the lease, Yagi asked his daughter Ritsuko to bring all of the furniture measurements into the space, and made sure that everything fit.

Undoubtedly the most impressive brought-in function is Prouvé's "sun shutter" from a Congo apartment facade. This aluminum structure separates the kitchen area from the main space with Prouvé's long glass "workshop table" that often holds a current project in process. Yagi was indeed impressed with this perfect fit, and explains how he actually uses it as a sun shutter. "The natural light is a strong factor here. We would like to put up more art like the San Francisco office, but the sun is too strong. Although now, we literary work with the light. We try to wrap up work when light goes from the office." Yagi still successfully gives a large space for art in the main space, where a unique installation by Mauro Giaconi, which the sun tan, tape stains and breeze movements are all part of the piece.

Yagi's studio is always lively with his staff, as well as a physical presence of a few projects at any given time. On his shelf, many inspiration pieces are adrift, such as birds'

eggs and nests, seed pods and living plants. "We also enjoy cooking here," explains Yagi, "for practical reasons too. You need to drive far, or worry about parking when taking a lunch break around here. Instead, we set a rule to cook and eat in an hour, and take turns in making lunch. The kitchen works really well once we got the hang of it. I feel that a good prepping job is equivalent to making good design decisions. Layout details and font decisions for example. A good cook may well be a good designer, you know?" The pickled cucumbers, eggs, and even sausages are evidences of the well used kitchen. Their own Kombucha is going below the counter too. The neighborhood farmers market happens every Friday, and they stock up weekly with the season's freshest ingredients. The popular menus are Pho Ga (Chicken noodle soup), Mapo Tofu (spicy bean paste tofu), Thai Curry, and grilled mackerel. Many conversations are exchanged over the meal and you can see how they could get obsessed with the process of certain specialties. This day, when we visited, one of the staff Shinsuke made a fresh pesto pasta. The Japanese earthenware mortar which was wrapped in cloth and stacked away in the cupboard, seems to be one of their favorite cooking tools. Originally made for Kyoto's buddhist temple, "they often make sesame tofu with this, but today we are making pesto. We blend together fresh basil, garic, pine nuts, Parmesan, olive oil and salt. It's as simple as that." The pestle moves at a steady pace, and within 20 minutes, the lunch is ready. Bright green sauce gets served in the white bowl, at which point you realize that the food is also a design happening on the plate.

With basic elements such as food and natural light passing through his studio, Yagi and his staff seem to embrace the subtle seasons that occur here in Los Angeles.

八木 保　*Tamotsu Yagi*

1984年にアパレルメーカー《ESPRIT》のアートディレクターに抜擢され渡米。91年に Tamotsu Yagi Design を設立し、アップルストアのコンセプトデザインなどを手がけた。現在は LA を拠点に活躍し、娘の理都子さんのデザインショップ『Chariots on Fire』で《TYZ (Tamotsu Yagi Zakka)》ブランドも展開している。

An art director originally from Japan, Yagi relocated his base in San Francisco to work with apparel company *ESPRIT* in 1984. In 1991, *Tamotsu Yagi Design (TYD)* was established, and has worked since on projects like Apple Store's concept design. His product line *TYZ (Tamotsu Yagi Zakka)* is showcased at his daughter Ritsuko Yagi's select store *Chariots on Fire*.

http://www.yagidesign.com   http://www.chariotsonfire.com

CHAPTER TWO. TOKYO

05 / 香菜子
Kanako

LOTA PRODUCT
Designer,
Illustrator
Setagaya-ku, Tokyo

広い庭付きのマンションは都内では希少。開放感のあるリビングには、光がたっぷり差し込む。仕事、家事、育児と
フル稼働の毎日で、日中の大半はここで過ごす。だからこそ、常に心地良い空間づくりを目指しているという

温もりを感じるアメリカンヴィンテージのソファとローテーブルは『アクメファニチャー』のもの。家具は旦那様がほとんど選ぶのだとか。
建物の周りをぐるりと囲む広い庭は、引っ越した当時、かなり和風なテイストだったが、自ら枕木を敷き、植栽し直した

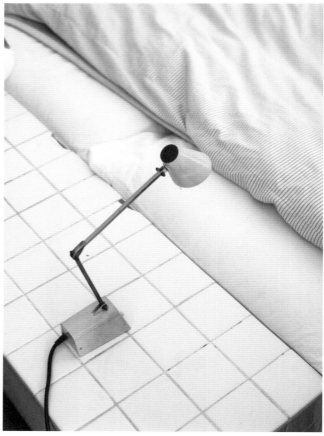

ドイツの照明デザイナー、インゴ・マウラーと妻のドロシー・ベッカーによる壁掛けの収納家具「ウーテンシロ」を
上手に使いこなしている香菜子さん。細々とした筆記用具からミニほうきまで、見せる収納のお手本になる

育児を通して見えてきた、
母親たちに寄り添うようなものづくりをしたい

　イラストレーター兼デザイナーで、最近モデルの仕事も復帰した香菜子さんは、中学生と小学生のお子さんを持つ2児の母。母親になってから感じた"欲しいもの"をかたちにすべく立ち上げた雑貨ブランド《LOTA PRODUCT》では、子育てに奮闘する母親たちに向けたアイテムを提案している。そんな香菜子さんが暮らすのは、世田谷区にある築30年ほど経た、落ち着いた佇まいのマンション。リビングの大きな窓と広い庭が開放感たっぷりで、気持ちの良い空間が広がる。「実はこの物件、売れ残っていたんです。最初に私が1人で見に来た時は、木が覆い茂っていて、暗くて、あまり印象が良くなかった。でも夫が見に来た際に広さに惚れてしまって。その後、壁全体を白く塗ったらいいかもしれないとなり、購入時に全面リフォームをしました。和風だった庭は植栽し直して、枕木を置いて。今、仕事場になっているデスクのある部屋はもともと茶室だったのですが、壁を抜きました。ここは仕事から家事へと、動線的にもちょうどいいんです」

　友人に作ってもらったという棚とデスクのあるスペースで仕事をこなす香菜子さんが《LOTA PRODUCT》として本格的に仕事をスタートしたのは、下のお子さんが生まれてから。「とにかく何かものを作りたいという思いがあったのと、第一子が生まれる前までモデルをやっていたのですが、妊娠してからはその仕事もなくなり、社会からスパっと切り離されたような、ものすごい孤独感を味わいました。そんな経験から、2人目の時はもうそれは嫌だなと思って、多少時間やお金がかかっても何かやっていかないとダメになると思っていました。ある程度子育ての要領もわかってきたし、余裕も出てきたということもあります」

　《LOTA PRODUCT》としては、最初に子供用の長めのエプロンを作った。「子供って基本的に汚しますよね。そういうことを怒りたくないというか、怒ることを減らしたくて。それが理由の一つとしてありました。下まで覆っている長めのエプロンだったら、ある程度汚れも防げる

し、こぼしてもそのついでに拭けるとか、母親が使うとしても機能的ですよね。短いエプロンってかわいいんですけど、全然長さが足りないんです(笑)」。そういった視点は子を持つ親ならでは。育児は楽しいだけではないということを、身をもって知っているからこそ、香菜子さんが手がけるアイテムには母親がふっと肩の力を抜くことができるような極めて優しい視点と気配りが随所に施されている。「環境や体に優しい蜜蝋キャンドルやソイキャンドルも作りました。あとはトートバッグを作ったり、メッセージバッジを作ったりとか。バッジには、"share""small"などのメッセージを入れているのですが、それを見て何か気づきになるようなものを作りたいと思ったんです。例えば"slow"だったら、少し歩みをゆるめてみようかなとか。そういうきっかけができるといいなと思って」

　仕事をしながら年中無休の母親業もこなす香菜子さんの毎日は忙しい。けれども「子供を持って、いろいろなことを同時にこなしたり、限られた時間の中で終わらせたりすることがすごく上手になりました。もともとできたわけではなく、できるようになったという感じです」。そして忙しいからこそ、毎日の暮らしを楽しむための工夫も忘れない。リビングの棚には子供たちの産着が入った透明なボトルをディスプレイしている。産院から出てきた時にいちばん最初に着せたものだという。細いラベルには、子供の名前と誕生日が。「染みができてどうしても抜けないものをわざと見えるように瓶に入れているんです。それを見るたびに当時のことを思い出します。タイムカプセルと一緒ですね」。ちょっとしたアイデアの積み重ねが日々の暮らしを豊かなものにしてくれる。

　「いろんなことを経験して、最近になって、やっぱりこれが好きなんだっていうのが見えてきました。そしたら、ものづくりにも迷いがなくなってきましたね」。気負うことなく、マイペースで好きなことに取り組んでいる香菜子さん。ものづくりのスピリットと暮らしのアイデアに溢れたライフスタイルが、ナチュラルな彼女の魅力を一層輝かせている。

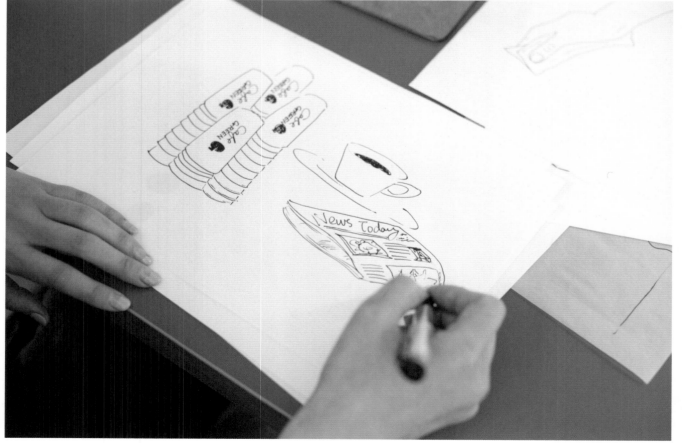

Parenthood the inspiration for products that give moms a helping hand

Kanako, an illustrator and designer who recently has also returned to modeling work, is the mother of two children, of junior high and elementary age. At *LOTA PRODUCT*, which she launched as a practical way to supply the things she came to feel, after becoming a parent, would be very handy to have, offers items for mothers tackling the day-to-day challenges of raising little ones.

Kanako lives in an elegant Setagaya apartment of over thirty years' vintage. The large living room window and generous garden give the home an airy, welcoming feel. According to Kanako, "When we bought the place we painted the walls white, and renovated throughout. We took out what was a Japanese-style garden and replanted, and put in railway sleepers. The room with the desk, which is now my work space, was a tea room, but we took out the wall. Doing so has also facilitated the ideal flow from work to domestic domain."

Harboring a desire to "just make something" as she raised the children, Kanako threw herself seriously into work after the birth of her second child. Her first creation was a long apron for children's use. "Basically, children will get grubby no matter what," she smiles. "One reason for designing the apron was that I didn't want to be telling them off for that sort of thing. A long apron that covers all the way down guards to some extent against getting dirty, and any mess can be wiped off, making it practical for moms too. Short aprons are cute, but they really don't cut the mustard," she laughs.

Plainly a parent's perspective, then. And of course, bringing up children is not all beer and skittles. Products supplied by Kanako's company are designed with a kindness and thoughtfulness that help take the weight off maternal shoulders. "We've also done beeswax candles and soy candles, gentle on the environment, and the body. And badges with words on them like "share" and "small." I wanted to make a thing that would bring something to people's attention when they saw it. For example, if the badge says "slow," maybe I should walk more slowly. It struck me as good to help people do those things."

Working and mothering – a fulltime job with no days off – means every day for Kanako is full on. But it's precisely because she's so busy that she finds ingenious ways to make day-to-day living more fun. On a shelf in the living room are clear bottles containing baby clothes belonging to her children. Kanako says these are what they were first dressed in after leaving the maternity hospital. Narrow labels give each child's name and date of birth. "I've put in the bottles clothes with stains that just won't come out, positioning them deliberately so that the marks are visible. When I see them it reminds me of that time. Like a time capsule, I suppose." One small idea, then another, and another, add up to make everyday living just that bit more varied and satisfying.

"Having experienced all sorts of things, recently I seem to have realized what it is I really like. And in turn, any uncertainty I had about making things has dissipated." Here is someone doing what she loves, at her own pace, without stress: a lifestyle overflowing with creative spirit and ideas for living causes this most natural of women to shine even brighter.

香菜子　*Kanako*

1975年、栃木県足利市生まれ。女子美術大学工芸科陶芸専攻卒業。在学中にモデルを始める。1998年、出産を機に引退。2005年、第二子出産を機に雑貨ブランド《LOTA PRODUCT（ロタ プロダクト）》を設立。母親の立場から「こんなものほしい」をかたちにすくデザインした雑貨が人気を集める。2008年よりイラストレーターとしての活動もスタート。また、モデル業も復帰し、さらなる活躍の場を広げている。2013年4月に刊行した初のコーディネートブックとなる『普段着BOOK』（主婦と生活社）が好評を博す。同年、10月には第2弾となる『普段着BOOK・秋冬』が刊行。

Born 1975 in Ashikaga, Tochigi. Worked as a fashion model while studying ceramic art at Joshibi University of Art and Design. In 1998, gave up modeling when pregnant with her first child. After giving birth to her second child in 2005, established *LOTA PRODUCT*, whose goods designed from a mother's viewpoint have garnered considerable attention. Starting work as an illustrator in 2008, and returning to modeling, she continues to diversify her career.

http://www.lotaproduct.com

06

相 場　正一郎

Shoichiro Aiba

LIFE / LIFE son Owner Chef
Shibuya-ku, Tokyo

《ケメックス》、《ストウブ》、ヴィンテージの《ル・クルーゼ》など、キッチンまわりの充実ぶりはさすが。アースカラーを中心とした配色のバランスも美しい

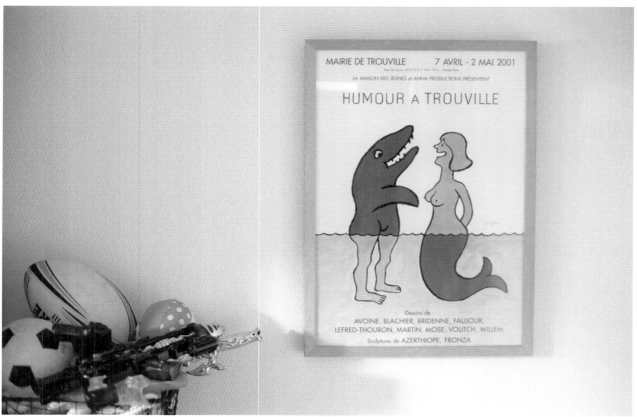

大阪の家具屋『TRUCK』は公私ともにお気に入り。自分たちで建物を建てる「セルフビルド」というコンセプトに影響
を受け、『LIFE』の内装の際に参考にした。プライベートでは、子供が生まれる時に特注で子供用のハイチェストを作っ
てもらったという。カメラをはじめ、趣味の多い相場さんの私物に囲まれて、子供たちのおもちゃもしっかりインテリアの
一部に。フランスの画家、レイモン・サヴィニャックのシュールでユーモラスなポスターが室内の雰囲気を和ませている

人とのつながりやコミュニティを大切にしながら
街のローカルな魅力を発信する

代々木公園に程近い、代々木八幡商店街にあるイタリアンレストラン『LIFE』と、2012年4月に参宮橋にオープンした『LIFE son』のオーナーシェフを務める相場正一郎さん。奥様と2人のお子さんと4人暮らしの相場さんの自宅は、そのふたつの店の中間あたり。山手通りから一本入った閑静な住宅街にある、築40年を超すヴィンテージマンションだ。「ここは本当に住みやすくて、これ以上の環境はないと思えるぐらい気に入っています。緑が多くて、故郷、栃木の田舎の風景に似ていて落ち着くんです」。大きなリビングに面したベランダから外を眺めると、都心とは思えないほど豊かな緑が広がっていて、森の中にいるように心地良い。家のあちらこちらには、ギターやカメラ、サーフボードやスケートボード、ラジコンなどが点在していて、仕事の合間に楽しむという趣味の多さに驚かされる。

毎日忙しく人気店を切り盛りする相場さんが、現在の職業を選んだのは自然な流れだった。「実家が総菜屋をやっていたこともあり、物心ついた頃から料理の道に進むものだと思っていました。伯父も田舎でログハウスを使った山小屋レストランをやっていて、その影響もあると思います」。高校卒業後、「若いうちに海外で武者修業してこい」という父親の勧めで単身イタリアに留学。イタリアでは、料理はもちろんのこと、技術以外に多くのことを学んだという。「家族が一番で、仕事は二の次、三の次。そういう考え方が基本にあって、家族を大切にする姿勢に影響を受けましたね。だからスタッフにも、家族や恋人との大事な予定がある場合は、休暇を取っていいよと言っています。あとは食卓を囲むとか、そういう場を大切にするということですね」

帰国後は原宿のレストランで店長として働き、その後、代々木八幡商店街に『LIFE』をオープンさせる。今でこそ同世代が営むカフェや飲食店が増えたが、当時は普通の商店街。勇気のいる決断だった。「正直、最初は不安もありました。でも最終的に決め手となったのは、父親のひとことでした。昔から店をやっていた父親を頼って、物件を一緒

に見てもらったんです。そうしたら、『この場所なら地元の人が来てくれる。間違いないだろ』と軽く言われて（笑）。それで、決心がつきましたね」。実際オープンしてからも「割とすぐに"町の食堂"という感じで、受け入れてもらえたんです」。地元のお客さんが定着してくれたので、幸運なことに経営面ではさほど苦労しなかったという。「イタリアンですが、ランチの付け合わせに父親の作ったひじきや切り干し大根を出しているんです。父親が『合うから』と無理矢理自分の惣菜を押し付けてきて（笑）、最初は渋々使っていたんですけど、評判が良くって」

ほとんどのお客さんが常連さんということにも頷ける。味に定評があるのはもちろんのこと、単なる"レストラン"にとどまらないのが『LIFE』の魅力でもある。「代々木公園を散歩して、帰りにウチでご飯を食べて、買い物に行く。お客さんがそんなコースを求めている気がしたので、周辺のお店も併せて紹介して喜んでもらえたらいいなと思って始めたんです」。編集者の山村光春さん（BOOKLUCK）と地元の情報を集積したフリーペーパー『PARK LIFE』を発行した。相場さん自身シェフという肩書きにとらわれることなく、マイペースで町に根ざした活動を行っている。「栃木の黒磯に『SHOZO』というカフェがあって、町づくりをコンセプトにしているんです。カフェブームなんていう言葉もない時代から、コミュニティを作ってきたオーナーの省三さんの考え方には、影響を受けていますね」

仕事もプライベートも家族や人とのつながりを大切にしてきた相場さん。最近周囲に同じような志を持ったお店が増えてきたこともあり、近隣ショップとローカルなイベントをもっと企画したいという。「何かしら動くことで、結果として町に還元できたらいいなと。特に代々木八幡や参宮橋は、渋谷や原宿といった繁華街とは違うし、代官山や自由が丘といった町とも違う。この地域ならではのコミュニティ感というか、心地良さみたいなものを、『LIFE』から発信していけたら、うれしいですね」

Cherishing connections and community to promote all that's good in the neighborhood

Shoichiro Aiba is owner chef of the Italian restaurant *LIFE* in Tokyo's Yoyogi-Hachiman retail district, and *LIFE son* that opened in Sangubashi in April 2012. The home Aiba shares with his wife and two children, situated about halfway between the two restaurants, is an apartment in a building that has stood for more than forty years in a quiet neighborhood off Yamate Dori. Aiba enthuses, "We love it round here, it's just such an easy place to live. With all the trees, it's like rural Tochigi where I grew up. Which makes me feel right at home." The view from the veranda off the large living room is far more verdant than one would normally expect in central Tokyo: like being in a forest, pleasant and relaxing. Scattered through the home are guitars and cameras, a surfboard and skateboard, radio-controlled toys... the owner chef manages to find time for a surprising number of hobbies in between his restaurant duties.

Aiba, whose busy daily round consists of managing his popular dining spots, came naturally to his present line of work. "My family had a sozaiya business (selling prepared dishes for customers to take home, deli-style), so from the time I was very young I just assumed I'd go into the cooking trade." After high school, at the suggestion of his father, who urged him to go and get some overseas training under his belt while he was still young, Aiba set out solo to study in Italy. From the Italians, he notes, he learned a lot, not only obviously about food and culinary techniques. "Basically, people there put family first, and work second or third. That family-first mentality had quite an impact on me."

On returning to Japan Aiba managed a restaurant in Harajuku, then opened *LIFE* in the Yoyogi-Hachiman shopping district. These days, there are more cafes and restaurants run by people around Aiba's age, but back then it was an ordinary shopping area, and siting the restaurant there was a leap of faith. But when his father, who had run his own business for decades, saw the property, he gave it his seal of approval, telling Aiba that in this location he couldn't fail. Now he was determined to make it work. And after actually opening, says Aiba, fortunately the restaurant escaped any major financial hiccups.

One can see why most of the customers are regulars. While naturally its food has an excellent reputation, part of *LIFE*'s allure is that it is more than just a restaurant. Refusing to be bound by the title of chef, Aiba also takes a wider role in the local community, as projects engage him. These include publishing *PARK LIFE*, a giveaway paper full of local news and information, in conjunction with editor Mitsuharu Yamamura (BOOKLUCK). "In Kuroiso in Tochigi there's a cafe called *Shozo*, the concept of which is building and empowering the local community. The approach of the owner, Shozo, who had worked to build up the community since before the idea of a 'cafe boom' even existed, has certainly influenced me."

In both his work and personal lives, Aiba has consistently made connecting with people top priority. Recently more and more businesses around him have begun to adopt the same philosophy, and he says he'd be keen to join with neighboring shops to organize local events. "The hope is that by initiating some sort of action, we can ultimately give back to the local area. Especially as places like Yoyogi-Hachiman and Sangubashi are different to big shopping districts like Shibuya and Harajuku. It'd be great to make *LIFE* the source of a sense of community if you like, a pleasurable vibe unique to this area."

相場 正一郎 *Shoichiro Aiba*

1975年、栃木県生まれ。総菜屋を営む両親のもとで育ち、18歳の時に修業のため単身イタリアへ留学。帰国後、原宿のレストラン勤務を経て、2003年に代々木八幡でイタリアンレストラン『LIFE』をオープンさせる。レシピ本の出版、フリーペーパーや雑誌、オリジナルプロダクトを制作するなど、幅広い活動が注目されている。2012年には参宮橋に姉妹店『LIFE son』もオープン。ふたつの店のキッチンに自らも立ち、メディア対応もこなすなど、多忙な日々を過ごす。

Born 1975 in Tochigi. Grew up with parents who ran a Japanese-style delicatessen, and moved to Italy at the age of eighteen to study cooking. On returning to Japan, worked at a restaurant in Harajuku. In 2003, opened his own Italian restaurant *LIFE* in Yoyogi-Hachiman. His diverse ventures include publishing cookbooks, free papers and magazines, and consistently attract wide-ranging attention. In 2012 opened his second restaurant, *LIFE son*, in Sangubashi.

http://www.s-life.jp

07

小林 和人
Kazuto Kobayashi

Roundabout / OUTBOUND Owner
Suginami-ku, Tokyo

「美術書や作品集などから何かしら影響を受けている」と話す小林さんの収集と陳列のアイデアソースは、ダダイズム
やロシア構成主義、フルクサスといった各国の芸術運動と前衛アーティストによるところが大きい。部屋にはヨーゼフ・
ボイス、クルト・シュヴィッタース、ハンス・アルプ、エル・リシツキー、サイ・トゥオンブリーなどの書籍が並ぶ

海外の蚤の市で見つけてきた古いものや現代作家による器などを配置。コーナーごとに緻密に計算されたディスプレイが秀逸

テーマは“収集と陳列”
ものの良さが際立つ最適な場所を探す

国内外から集めた日用品や道具、オブジェなどを扱う、吉祥寺のセレクトショップ『Roundabout』と『OUTBOUND』。両店のオーナーである小林和人さんは、吉祥寺から少し離れた閑静な住宅街に奥様と2人のお子さんと暮らしている。生い茂った木々の隙間から覗く一軒家は、木のぬくもりのある山小屋のような佇まいでありながら、ほど良くモダンな印象を放っている。「不動産屋さんから面白い物件があると紹介してもらったのがこの家でした。内見をした際、2階に上がったら部屋に気持ちの良い光が入っていて、そこで新生活のイメージが湧いたんです。最初は木の壁の家に住むという発想はなかったのですが、とにかく居心地が良くて。いい具合になじんだ古着みたいな良さを感じています」

かねてよりショップのディスプレイに定評のある小林さん。居住空間にも独創的な世界観が漂う。「店と自宅に置いてあるものはそんなに違いはないですが、とにかく店の商品に関しては妥協したくなくて（笑）。以前は、家に置くのはもったいないというか、それだったら店を充実させたいという気持ちが強かった。今は“店主のプライベートの充実”というのがまずあって、店はそのフィードバックであるべきと思うようになりました」

部屋中をぐるりと見回すと、いろいろな“もの”があるが雑然としていない。棚いっぱいのレコードやアーティストの洋書、店でも取扱いのある作家ものの器やオブジェなどが小気味良く配置されている。「ものの良さが際立つ場所を探すのが自分の役目なので、置いては外してというのを繰り返して、最適な場所を探すことを大事にしています。私のテーマは“収集と陳列”。『Roundabout』のオープン直後は、本当はこうしたいという漠然としたビジョンがありながらも、現状の品物ではどうやっても思い描いている画には近づけなかったんです。それでも夜な夜なディスプレイ替えを繰り返しやったことが良いトレーニングになっていたのかもしれません。無意識的な反復練習です。自分の中で違和感を感じるか、心地良く落ちるかという部分で判断します。それは

今でも変わらないですね」

1999年、大学卒業直後に友人らと始めた『Roundabout』。その後、メンバーはそれぞれやりたい方向へと別れていき、2000年に1人になった。「仲間と始められたのも良かったし、結果的に1人になったのも今では良かった」という。2008年には「路面店としてかなり理想的なロケーション」と出会い、2店舗目の『OUTBOUND』をスタート。具体的な機能を持った道具や日用品を扱う『Roundabout』とは対照的に、こちらでは日常使いとは言い切れないものも提案。もののもつ「余白」から生まれる豊かさや安らぎといった目に見えない作用を感じてほしいという。折しも手仕事のきめ細かさへの興味も徐々に大きくなってきた頃だった。

「『Roundabout』にそういった視点を入れ込もうとも思いましたが、元々あったかもしれないラフな良さが失われて、店として整いすぎてしまうのではないかという危惧がありました。アーティストの大竹伸朗さんが本の中で“雑の領域”という言葉を使っていて、それは、完成しきっていない、判断保留の状態を残したものの良さだと勝手に解釈しているんですけど、そういった切りっぱなしの要素を保っていきたいと思いました。異なる温度の店を作ることによって頭の中の引き出しを分けたということなのかもしれません」

日常と非日常を楽しむ、両店舗とも考え尽くされたコンセプトがショップの人気を支えている。「いわゆるデザイナーものをただ有名だからと置いている店というのは、全く興味ないですね。やっている人の視点とか切り口が匂わないと、どうしても共感できる余地を見つけられないんです。著名なデザイナーものがありつつ、アノニマスなものがある。あるいは、逆に特定の時代や一人のデザイナーへの偏愛でも、店主の編集眼が感じられるお店が良いですね」

独自の審美眼が遺憾なく発揮された空間で、丁寧に言葉を選びながら話してくれた小林さん。並々ならぬこだわりから、一つ一つのものたちに注がれる愛情の深さが垣間見えた気がした。

「『OUTBOUND』は緊張感があってすっきりした空間に、『Roundabout』は蚤の市で
掘り出し物を探すような楽しみがある場所であってほしい」とは小林さん。その両方を
兼ね備えているかのような自宅は、にぎやかでありながら静謐さが漂う

"Collecting and displaying" is his theme;
Finding the spot to show a thing off to best advantage, his role

Roundabout and *OUTBOUND* are popular stores dealing in everyday necessities, tools and utensils, art objects and so on, Japanese and imported. Kazuto Kobayashi, owner of both stores, lives with his wife and two children in a quiet residential neighborhood not far from Kichijoji. The house, just visible through a gap in dense foliage, uses a lot of wood in its exterior cladding, giving it the air of a mountain hut, yet at the same time the mortar walls visible in parts provide just the right impression of modernity. "The estate agent told us he had an interesting property on the books, and showed us this. The idea of living in a house with timber walls had never occurred to us, but actually it's very comfortable, like an old familiar piece of clothing perfectly worn in."

Kobayashi has long had a reputation for his shop displays, and this creative worldview obviously extends to the family's living space. Looking around one finds all sorts of "stuff," yet nowhere feels cluttered. The shelves of records, books on artists, pots, art objects etc. made by artists stocked by the stores are all neatly arranged. Kobayashi explains, "Looking for the place that will show a thing off to best advantage is my role, so I put it down, then take it away, over and over until I find the right spot. Finding that perfect spot is vital for me. 'Collecting and displaying' is my thing. Just after *Roundabout* opened, I had a vision of what I really wanted to do, but didn't manage to achieve anything like the image in my head. Still, I suppose all those nights spent altering the displays over and over did turn out to be good training. It comes down to whether something sits comfortably, or doesn't feel quite right. I guess that will always be the case."

Kobayashi started Roundabout with friends soon after graduating from university in 1999. In 2008 he found what he describes as "pretty much the ideal location for a high-street operation," and opened his second store, *OUTBOUND*. In contrast to *Roundabout*, which deals in practical utensils, everyday homewares etc. *OUTBOUND* also offers items that could hardly be described as for everyday use. Kobayashi says he wants people to sense the invisible effects, the richness and relaxation born out of the "blank space" in things. "I did consider taking a similar approach to Roundabout as well, but there was a risk of the store losing what may have been its original rough, intriguingly jumbled look, and becoming too orderly. So by creating two stores of different 'ambient temperature,' so to speak, you might say I've compartmentalized in my own mind."

The popularity of the stores is underpinned in both cases by a carefully cultivated concept of celebrating both ordinary and extraordinary. "I've no interest whatsoever in shops that just carry so-called designer goods because they're famous," says Kobayashi. "Without some whiff of how the person running the store sees things, or their approach to things, it's hard for me to find anything to relate to. Shops with goods by well-known designers, but also anonymous things: these are good. Or conversely, even if it favors a particular era or designer, a shop where you get a sense of the owner's eye for bringing things together."

Sitting in surroundings that give full play to his own distinctive aesthetic, Kobayashi chose his words carefully, his extraordinary attention to detail offering a glimpse of the great affection he feels toward every object in his home.

小林 和人　*Kazuto Kobayashi*

1975年、東京都生まれ。幼少期をオーストラリアとシンガポールで過ごす。1999年、多摩美術大学卒業後、国内外の生活用品を扱う店『Roundabout（ラウンダバウト）』を吉祥寺にて始める。2008年には、やや非日常に振れた品々を展開するショップ『OUTBOUND（アウトバウンド）』をスタート。両店舗のすべての商品のセレクトと店内のディスプレイ、年数回のベースで開催される展覧会の企画を手がける。スタイリングや執筆もこなす。著書に『あたらしい日用品』（マイナビ）がある。

Born 1975 in Tokyo. After graduating from Tama Art University in 1999, opened the *Roundabout* store selling Japanese and imported homewares, in Kichijoji. In 2008 started *OUTBOUND*, a shop stocking the slightly out of the ordinary. Responsible for selecting all merchandise for both stores, instore displays, and planning exhibitions held several times a year. Author of *Atarashii Nichiyohin* (New items for everday use; Mynavi)

http://roundabout.to   http://outbound.to

08 / 光石 研
Ken Mitsuishi

Actor
Setagaya-ku, Tokyo

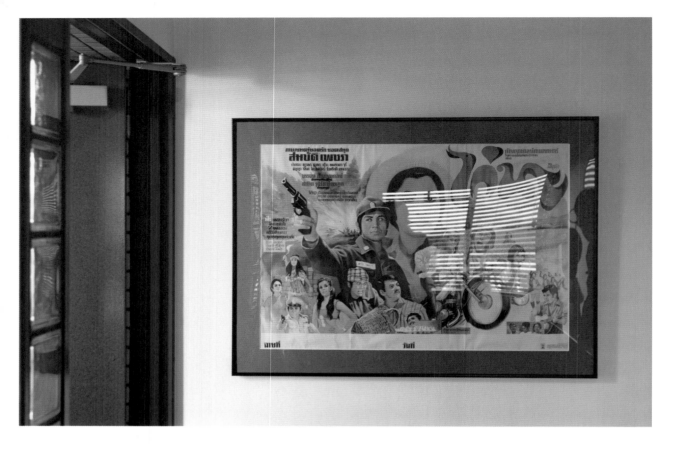

格子のついたガラスの扉は、かつて青山にあった『イデー』のショップで使われていたものと同じデザイン。三角に抜けた
天井が開放感をもたらすリビングには、長年少しずつ集めてきたこだわりの家具たちが揃う。中でも黒いアイアンのオブ
ジェに心惹かれるという。セルジュ・ムーユのランプは一灯と三灯を所有。愛用しているソファとテーブルは『パシフィッ
クファニチャーサービス』のもの。昔からインテリアが大好きだった

機材がぴったり収まるように別注で作ったレコード棚。お気に入りの50年代〜70年代のソウルミュージックのレコードがぎっしり

海外によく行くようになってから、アメリカンフィフティーズよりヨーロッパやフレンチフィフティーズものが増えた。最近気になるのはタイのインテリア

郵便はがき

1 7 0 8 7 9 0

038

料金受取人払郵便

豊島局承認

7732

差出有効期間
平成28年1月
14日まで

東京都豊島区南大塚2-32-4
パイ インターナショナル 行

‖‖‖·‖·‖‖·‖·‖‖‖·‖·‖·‖‖‖·‖·‖·‖·‖·‖·‖·‖·‖·‖·‖·‖·‖·‖‖

書籍をご注文くださる場合は以下にご記入ください

●小社書籍のご注文は、下記の注文欄をご利用下さい。**宅配便の代引**にてお届けします。代引手数料と
送料は、ご注文合計金額（税抜）が3,000円以上の場合は無料、同未満の場合は代引手数料300円（税
抜）、送料200円（税抜・全国一律）。乱丁・落丁以外のご返品はお受けしかねますのでご了承ください。

●**お届け先は裏面に**ご記載ください。
　（発送日、品切れ商品のご連絡をいたしますので、必ずお電話番号をご記入ください。）

●電話やFAX、小社WEBサイトでもご注文を承ります。
　http://www.pie.co.jp　TEL：03-3944-3981　FAX：03-5395-4830

ご注文書籍名	冊数	税込価格
	冊	円
	冊	円
	冊	円
	冊	円

ご購入いただいた本のタイトル

●普段どのような媒体をご覧になっていますか？（雑誌名等、具体的に）

　雑誌（　　　　　　　　　　　　　）　WEBサイト（　　　　　　　　　　　）

●この本についてのご意見・ご感想をお聞かせください。

●今後、小社より出版をご希望の企画・テーマがございましたら、ぜひお聞かせください。

フリガナ お名前	男 ・ 女	西暦 　　　　　年　　　　月　　　　日生　　　歳
ご住所（〒　　　　　－　　　　　　）　　TEL		
e-mail		
ご職業		

お客様のご感想を新聞等の広告媒体や、小社Facebook・Twitterに匿名で紹介させていただく場合がございます。不可の場合のみ「いいえ」に○を付けて下さい。	いいえ

使い古された味のあるものが好き、
結果的にそういうものが集まっている

俳優歴35年、日本映画界屈指のバイプレイヤーとして知られる光石研さん。映画だけでも出演本数は150本以上、市井の人から極道まで、全く違う役柄に変幻自在する、生粋の名役者である。そのご自宅は、世田谷区の閑静な住宅街に佇む瀟洒なマンション。天井を抜いて開放感を演出した室内など、リフォームのアイデアは、すべて光石さん本人が考えたものだ。

「まずはここを買う前に、天井が抜けるかどうかを確認しました。それで、スケルトンにして、床をはってもらって、カウンターを付けて……。最初は予算もないから手つかずのところもあって、後からリフォームしました。そうやって少しずつ手を加えていければいいと思ったんです」。リフォーム時には、自分の目指す内装プランを実現するためにノートを1冊作ったという。「雑誌のキリヌキを貼って『この床はこんな感じ』とか『ここは白く塗って』と自分の理想のイメージを伝えるために、かなり細かく指定しました」。天井には、部分的にコンクリート打ちっぱなしのままの箇所がある。「綺麗に直すのはいつでもできるし、ボルトや数字などラフな感じが良くて、痕跡を残そうとそのままにしておいてもらったんです。でも義父が来た時に『まだ途中か?』って言っていましたけど(笑)」

こだわって手に入れた空間には、随所に愛着のある椅子やオブジェ、レコードなど、お気に入りのものたちがディスプレイされている。インテリアやファッション、音楽が好きな光石さんが一番影響を受けたのは、ティーンエイジャーのころに訪れたフィフティーズブームだ。「特に古着屋にはしょっちゅう行っていましたね。その流れでインテリアも中古家具に興味を持って。昔、古着屋で『クリームソーダ』という店があって、そこが今の裏原宿に『ガレッヂパラダイス東京』という店を作って2階に家具を売っていたんです。民家を真っ白に塗った店で、アメリカの中古家具を売っていて、それがカッコ良くて。当時はお金がなかったから買えなかったんですけど、憧れでした」

今でも有名無名関係なくいろいろな家具屋に行くという。東京だけなく、仕事で訪れる地方や旅先の海外でもチェックは欠かさない。でもやはり、好きなのは新しいものより古いもの。「あまりキラキラしたものよりは、使い古された味のあるもの、少し手あかのついたくらいの方が好きで、結果的にそういうものが集まっていますね」

直感のおもむくままに椅子や小物を購入することが多いが、特に家具は洋服と違って、購入した時のエピソードをよく覚えているという。「プルーヴェっぽい、と思って目に留まった椅子は明治通り沿いの洋服屋にあったものを譲ってもらいました。ブラジルのデザイナーのリプロダクションである『コンプレックス』のスパイチェアは、一目見て購入。イームズのロッキングチェア(RAR)は、現在青山にある『ビオトープ』のオーナーさんが昔、下北沢で働いていたお店で買ったんです。ダイニングの照明は、奥さんが世田谷通り沿いの古道具屋さんで見つけたものだし、バーカウンターにあるスツールは50年代のアメリカのもので、下北沢のジャンクな店で。これ両手に抱えて、電車に乗って持って帰ってきましたよ(笑)」

そんな数あるインテリアの中でも、一番思い入れのあるものが「廊下とリビングを結ぶ、格子のついたガラスの扉」。それはかつて青山にあった『イデー』のお店で使われていたものだ。当時一目惚れした光石さんは、「こっそり携帯で撮った(笑)」。その後、偶然の巡り合わせで、その扉を作った本人と会うことができ、同じものを作ってもらったという。日々の暮らしを彩るような家具やものたちを、長年にわたって少しずつ集めてきた光石さん。今はお気に入りに囲まれて毎日過ごすことができることが何より幸せと笑う。「結局好きなものって、10代から何も変わっていないんです。今後もおそらく変わらないですね」

それぞれにストーリーのあるインテリア。部屋中に流れるソウルミュージックのBGMと相まって、そこにはいつも気持ちよく柔らかな時間が流れている。

Love for the worn and well-loved leads to a home full of exactly that

A stalwart of Japanese cinema for 35 years now, Ken Mitsuishi is known as one of the country's most outstanding supporting actors. With over 150 film roles alone to his name, Mitsuishi is an actor's actor with a chameleon-like ability to transform himself into completely different characters, from everyman to hardened criminal. Home is an elegant apartment in a quiet Setagaya neighborhood. All alterations to the apartment, such as removing ceilings to give an airier, more spacious feel, spring from Mitsuishi's own ideas. For the alterations he apparently compiled a book of notes to ensure the interior would look the way he wanted, sticking in magazine clippings and personally directing the building work with some precision.

Parts of the ceiling still have exposed concrete. According to Mitsuishi, "Those sections can be tidied up anytime we want, and actually we like that rough unfinished look with the bolts and numbers etc. so had them deliberately leave it like that, to show where the building work had been done. Mind you, when my father-in-law came he wondered if we still hadn't finished (laughs)."

All over the spaces achieved by such obsessive attention to detail, Mitsuishi displays his favorite things: well-loved chairs, art objects, records. A fan of interior design, fashion and music, Mitsuishi's greatest influence has been the '50s craze that swept Japan in his teenage years. He began to frequent second-hand clothing shops, leading in turn to a fascination with second-hand interior goods. And he still prefers old to new, noting, "We like things with a well-worn feel to them, things that look like they've been handled a bit, to the brand spanking new, so we've ended up with a home full of exactly those things."

He tends to pick up the likes of chairs and small items on impulse, and says that particularly with furniture, unlike clothing, he often remembers the stories behind his purchases.

"There's the chair I asked someone to pass on, that caught my eye because it looked like a Prouvé, and the spy chair from *Complex* that I spied and had to have right then and there. The Eames rocking chair (RAR) is from a shop that was in Shimokitazawa years ago. The light fixtures in the dining room my wife found at a second-hand appliance shop on Setagaya-dori, while the bar stools came from a junk shop in Shimokitazawa. I carried them home on the train, tucked under each arm (laughs)."

Of all the items in the apartment, Mitsuishi says the most thought went into the latticed glass door connecting hallway and living room. It's the door that used to be in the *IDÉE* shop in Aoyama. Love at first sight was followed by obsession, then by pure coincidence an encounter with the person who made the *IDÉE* door. Mitsuishi promptly commissioned an identical one. Slowly, over the years, Mitsuishi has accumulated furniture and objects that add color to day-to-day living, and now admits with a smile that nothing beats spending every day surrounded by one's favorite things. "In the end, I still love the same things I did as a teenager. And I don't imagine that will change anytime soon."

Interior goods each with their own story are the perfect complement to the soul music that drifts through the apartment, all adding up to a mellow, feelgood time, all the time.

光石 研　*Ken Mitsuishi*

1961年、福岡県生まれ。高校在学中に受けたオーディションで主役に抜擢され、78年に映画『博多っ子純情』(曾根中生監督)でデビュー。以来、映画、テレビ、CMなどに数多く出演。サラリーマンのお父さんからヤクザまで、多様なキャラクターを演じ分ける。主な出演作は、『Helpless』(96年・青山真治監督)、『紀子の食卓』(06年・園子温監督)、『あぜ道のダンディ』(11年・石井裕也監督)。最近では、『ヒミズ』(12年・園子温監督)、『アウトレイジ ビヨンド』(12年・北野武監督)、『共喰い』(13年・青山真治監督)など話題作に出演。

Born 1961 in Fukuoka. Cast through an audition attended while in high school, he made his film debut in 1978 playing the lead in *Hakatakko Junjo* (directed by Chusei Sone). Has since appeared in numerous films, TV series and ads, as an array of characters ranging from office-worker dad to yakuza. Major film appearances include *Helpless* (1966, directed by Shinji Aoyama), *Noriko's Table* (2006, directed by Sion Sono), *A Man with Style* (2011, directed by Yuya Ishii) and most recently, *Himizu* (2012, directed by Sion Sono), *Outrage Beyond* (directed by Takeshi Kitano), and *Tomogui* (2013, directed by Shinji Aoyama).

http://www.dongyu.co.jp

09 / 滝沢 時雄　滝沢 緑
Tokio Takizawa, Midori Takizawa

The Conran Shop Buyer, Klala Owner
Kawasaki, Kanagawa

この家の決め手は、光の入り具合と豊富なグリーンに囲まれていること。光のたっぷり入るキッチンに立つことが多くなったという緑さん。《ターク》のフライパンや柳宗理のキッチンツールなどお気に入りを揃える。一方、時雄さんは木々の生い茂った中庭がお気に入り。四季や時間の流れを感じられるような空間を探していたという

床、壁、ドア、室内の窓枠など、ディテールにこだわったリノベーション。リビングの扉はフランスのアンティーク。ベッドルームの扉は1920年代のイギリス製。なかなか気に入ったものが見つからない中で出会った、思い入れのある扉。ベッドルームはシンプルでクリーンな印象。《トーネット》の椅子と『エースホテル』のベッドカバーでシックにコーディネート

ミッドセンチュリーとアンティーク、
インダストリアル系との組み合わせの妙を楽しむ

インテリアショップの『ザ・コンランショップ』で家具、雑貨のバイイングを担当している滝沢時雄さんと、雑貨を中心としたセレクトショップ『klala』の店主を務める滝沢緑さん。ともにインテリアの仕事に関わる夫妻の自宅は、建築家の内井昭蔵が設計した、築40年ほど経たヴィンテージマンション。もともと時雄さんの会社の同僚がこのマンションに住んでいたという。「遊びに行ったときに、間取りと雰囲気がいいなと思って。その後、空き物件があると知り、内見して即決しました」。窓枠のサイズからベランダの形状、物干し竿を引っ掛けるフレームまで、随所にこだわりを感じさせる。時雄さん曰く「内井昭蔵さんのデザインはディテールが面白いんです。特徴的なのが、収納が全部外に出ていて、居室スペースが広く使えるところ。縦長の物件では、縦部分の南側に開口があるのが一般的ですが、この物件は贅沢に横部分の広い面に窓があるんです。前の家は日当たりが良くなかったので、とにかく光の入り方というのがポイントでした。寝室に内窓を付けたのも空間に連続性を持たせたかったという狙いがあります」

リノベーションの際には、施主が設計などに参加できる業者を選んだ。「自分で設計して、パーツも揃えて、現場の進捗を見ながら決めていきたくて。実際は仕事が忙しくなってしまい、95%はお任せしてしまいましたが（笑）。特にこだわったのは床です。オークで幅広の床材を探して。節とか割れとか全部ひっくるめて自然なものが良かったんです。残念ながら床張りはできませんでしたが、床のオイルは自分で塗りましたし、壁も業者さんと一緒に作ることができて楽しかったですね」と時雄さん。もともと美容師をしていた時雄さんがインテリア業界に入るきっかけとなったのは、お客さんが装丁していた『SANTA FE STYLE』(Christine Mather)という1冊の本と出会ったことから。「初めて目にしてから、すっかり感化されてしまいました。壁とドアの色のコントラストとかが良くて。壁の飾り方なんかも、コンランのスタイルと共通していますね。あとは『Mid-Century Modern: Furniture of the 1950s』(Cara Greenberg)。これは古い家具を好きになるきっかけとなった本です。僕のベースはやはりミッドセンチュリーのデザインなんです」。実際にヨーロッパのアンティークやジャン・プルーヴェのテーブル、《ジェルデ》のライトといったインダストリアル系をミッドセンチュリーの家具と組み合わせた室内は、古いものが持つ温もりを一層感じられる空間になっている。

一方、こだわりの強い時雄さんとは対照的にリノベーションについてのこだわりはほとんどなかったという緑さん。けれども「収納の多さだけはリクエストしました。前の家は収納が少なくて、ものがいつも出ているような状態だったんです。仕事でもいろいろなものが溢れている状態なので、家はホテルみたいに何もない状態にしたくて。それ以外はお好きにどうぞって（笑）」。現在、緑さんは国内外の雑貨や器、オブジェなどを中心に日々の暮らしに彩りを与えてくれるようなアイテムを展開する『klala』のオーナー。2005年にネットショップからスタートし、当時は旅先で買った北欧のアンティーク食器やフランスの絵本など、個人的にいろいろ集めていたものを売っていた。手応えを感じたところで、2010年、世田谷区太子堂にリアルショップを構えた。これまでいろいろなものに触れてきたが、セレクトの基準はほとんど直感だという。そして、お店では自分たちの好きなアイテムだけを売ろうと決めているのだとか。「古いものと新しいものを生活の中にうまく取り入れられるように」、それが品揃えのテーマであり、彼らのライフスタイルの基盤となっている。

ここに引越しをしてから生活のサイクルも変わり、これからはもっと自宅でゆっくり過ごす時間を大切にしたいという2人。中庭の木々の葉を初夏の清々しい風が揺らし、室内を柔らかい光が包み込む。「実は今まで家で過ごす時間が少なくて料理と疎遠になりがちだったのですが、このキッチンはまた料理をしたいという気持ちになるから不思議です」。光がふんだんに差し込むキッチンに立った緑さんがやさしく微笑む姿が印象的だった。

Savoring a superb combination of mid-century, antique, and industrial

Tokio Takizawa is a buyer of furniture and homewares for *The Conran Shop* interior design store. Midori Takizawa manages *klala*, a select shop focusing mainly on homewares, gifts, and general merchandise. The home of this couple both working in interiors is a "vintage" apartment about forty years old, designed by architect Shozo Uchii. Attention to detail is evident throughout the residence, from the size of the window frames to the shape of the veranda, and the frame holding the poles used for drying laundry. According to Tokio, "Shozo Uchii's designs are fascinating in their detail. Most distinctively, storage is all external, freeing up plenty of living room space inside. Usually in a long, narrow property like this, the openings are on the shorter south side, but here, rather more generously, the windows are on the longer, larger side. Our previous home was not well positioned for sun, so the way the light comes in here was a definite plus for us. We installed an internal window in the bedroom to create spatial continuity."

When it came to renovating the apartment, the Takizawas chose a contractor who was happy to have owner input into the design. According to Tokio, "We were especially particular about the floors, and went looking for wide oak flooring, preferably natural with all the knots, splits and so on." Tokio, originally a hairdresser, got into the interior trade after coming across Christine Maher's book *Santa Fe Style*, for which one of his customers did the cover design. "The moment I set eyes on that book, I was inspired. Aspects such as the contrasting colors of walls and doors were imprinted on my consciousness instantly. Another influence was *Mid-Century Modern: Furniture of the 1950s* (Cara Greenberg). This was the book that sparked my love of antiques. I like the Scandinavians, but must admit, always come back to mid-century design."

The interior of the apartment, which actually combines European antiques and mid-century furniture, only serves to highlight the warmth of old things.

In contrast to Tokio with his strong preferences, Midori says there was nothing particular that she really wanted from the renovations. She does note however that "the one thing I did request was lots of storage space. At work we're always overflowing with stuff, so at home I wanted it to be bare, like a hotel. So I said let me have that, and for the rest, you can do what you like (laughs)." Formerly employed at *The Conran Shop*, Midori now manages *klala*, which stocks mainly homewares, tableware, art objects and so on, both Japanese and imported. Apparently the rule at the shop is to only sell the things they like, the things they want to sell. The store is stocked with a selection that allows customers to "incorporate both old and new in their lifestyles," and is the basis of their own personal lifestyle.

Since moving here the rhythm of the couple's life has also changed, the pair saying they want to now spend more time taking it easy at home. "Actually up to now we've spent very little time at home, and tended not to cook, but amazingly, this kitchen makes you want to cook." Midori with her quiet smile made a striking figure standing in that sundrenched space.

滝沢 時雄　*Tokio Takizawa*

栃木県生まれ。美容師を経て、1996年から『ザ・コンランショップ』勤務。2005年、北欧やヨーロッパをはじめ国内外の雑貨を集めた『klala（クララ）』をネットショップにてスタート。2010年には世田谷区太子堂に実店舗をオープンさせる。現在は『ザ・コンランショップ』と『klala』のバイイングを担当。

Born in Tochigi Prefecture. After working as a hairdresser, joined *The Conran Shop* in 1996. In 2005, launched the internet-based shop *klala*, offering a collection of Japanese and imported homewares, in 2005, and the real *klala* shop in 2010. Currently acts as a buyer for both *The Conran Shop* and *klala*.

滝沢 緑　*Midori Takizawa*

東京都生まれ。『ザ・コンランショップ』勤務後、2006年に株式会社ミナに入社。現在は週2日ほど『ミナ・ペルホネン』に勤務しながら『klala』の店主を務める。

Born in Tokyo. After working at *The Conran Shop*, joined *mina perhonen* in 2006. Currently works two days a week for *mina* while managing *klala*.

http://www.conran.co.jp　http://www.klala.net

10 / 鈴木 修司
Shuji Suzuki

B:MING LIFE STORE by BEAMS Buyer
Kamakura, Kanagawa

庭には厨子甕（ずしがめ）という沖縄の骨壺ややちむんが無造作に置かれ、独特の世界観が漂う。ダイニングチェアは《松本民芸家具》のラダーバックチェア

編組品と呼ばれるかご類を、さまざまな国や地方から集めて自在にディスプレイ。セルジュ・ムーユのランプ、ビューロートレビエとの相性も抜群

日常使いの器より、土瓶や飾り用の大皿など、造形的に魅力ある大きなものが好きだという鈴木さん。中でも小鹿田焼は「ものの魅力が圧倒的」だとか

ブルーノ・マットソンのアームチェアをはじめ、北欧アイテムも空間になじむ。現在は、ラトビアやハンガリー、ルーマニアなど東欧の手仕事に興味があるという

自分が家を建てる時は
『もやい工藝』のような造りにしようと決めていた

温暖な気候と豊かな自然に恵まれ、古都の風情ある街並みが、かねてより老若男女から愛されてきた鎌倉。その鎌倉の高台の一角に、セレクトショップ『BEAMS』に勤務する鈴木修司さんの新築の日本家屋がある。「高台で裏に山を背負っていたこと。それから、土地を見に来た時、庭の梅の木が満開で住みたくなってしまった」と笑う鈴木さんは、土地選びに始まり、家の構造から梁や床、建具といったパーツまで、すべて自分も参加して決めたという。

生活の中心となる2階は、梁をむき出しにして天井を高くし、たっぷりの採光を確保。「リビングはパブリックスペースなので、あまり古風な感じになりすぎないよう意識しました。天井の梁は飛騨高山のものです。この家を建てるにあたって、梁や建具を大工さんや設計士の方々と一緒に買いに行きました」。風通しの良い空間のいたるところにディスプレイされているのは、鈴木さんが愛してやまない民藝品やクラフトの数々。手仕事が光る逸品たちは、日本各地を旅しながらコツコツと蒐集してきたものだ。「日常使いの器より、土瓶や飾り用の大皿など、造形的に魅力ある大きなものが好きです。例えば、小鹿田焼だったら坂本茂木さん。かつてバーナード・リーチの付き添いをされていたような方で、今はもう現役を退かれていますが、坂本さんの器は僕の宝物ですね。沖縄のやちむんだと山田真萬さんや松田共司さん。倉敷ガラスの小谷真三さんの作品も多いです」

鈴木さんが民藝に興味を持ったのは、『BEAMS』の店舗で扱っていた出西窯の湯のみを手に取ったことから。その後、すっかりハマってしまい、日本全国の民藝店に足を運んだという。焼き物から入り、徐々にガラスや布、編組品と言われる樹皮や竹細工も好むようになっていった。「どこか日本の民族性を感じさせるようなプリミティブなモノが好きなんです」。そんな流れから、鎌倉にある民藝店『もやい工藝』のオーナー久野恵一さんと仲良くなった。やがてプライベートで久野さんの仕入れや買い付けについていくように。日本全国を一緒に旅しながら、生産者や職人と会い、窯を訪ねた。「久野さんはもともと民俗学を学ばれていたので、仕入れだけでなく、現地調査のやり方も教えてくれました。自分の後を継いでいくだろう若い世代の一人という感じで考えてくださっているようです。ある意味で一番弟子かもしれませんね（笑）。そんなつながりで、以前から『もやい工藝』の建物に憧れていたこともあって、自分が家を建てる時は絶対こういう感じにしようと決めていました」

当時、鈴木さんが購入する土地を決めたことを久野さんに報告すると、その場ですぐに設計士に連絡を取ってくれたという。監修に久野さん、数寄屋建築や日本の伝統的な建物を熟知している設計士さんと鎌倉で有名な大工さんという『もやい工藝』の建物を建てたかつてのチームが23年ぶりに再結成した。鈴木さんも設計のアイデアには積極的にかかわったという。「方眼紙を買ってきて、手書きで試行錯誤しながら何度も考えました。間取りは家族と決めたので、方眼紙に書いたものがそのままの家になった感じです。それから、ぼくは河井寛次郎が好きで、この家を建てるにあたって、京都の河井寛次郎記念館にも何度か足を運びました。階段など、ちょっと参考にしているところがあります」。中でも一番こだわった点は、「"朝鮮張り"にした2階の床です。朝鮮張りとは、均一の種類の長さや太さの材を揃えられなかった李朝時代の貧しい庶民が編み出した工法で、長い竿と言われる部分に、短い板を差し込んでいく板間の張り方のことを言うのですが、どうしてもこのスタイルでやりたかったんです」

こだわりが余すところなく凝縮された家。それら造形物の美しさを、一つ一つ丁寧に説明してくれる鈴木さん。「一年中庭にグリーンが欲しいので、これから常緑樹を植えようかと。それを楽しむ縁側も欲しいですね」。居を構えて3年、巡る季節とともに、これからも少しずつ手を加えていく喜びがある。四季折々の自然と手仕事のぬくもりに囲まれた新しい日本家屋スタイル。窓の外に目を向けると、庭にある梅の花がちらほらとほころび始めていた。

When it came to building his own house, he was determined to make it like Moyaikogei

With its congenial climate and verdant surroundings, Japan's ancient capital of Kamakura is loved by young and old. Tucked away on a slope in Kamakura stands the new traditionally Japanese-style home of Shuji Suzuki, who works for lifestyle store *BEAMS*. Suzuki chose everything himself: starting with the site and including the structure of the house and even its various components – rafters, floors, fittings – recalling with a laugh, "It was on a rise with hills behind. And when I came to check out the site, the garden had a plum tree in full bloom. How could I resist?!"

The second-floor living room on which day-to-day life centers features a high ceiling with exposed beams, and captures generous amounts of light. Suzuki accompanied the carpenter to buy the beams from Hida-Takayama. Displayed throughout the airy space are myriad examples of Suzuki's adored folk art and craftworks, exquisitely handcrafted treasures accumulated on travels around the country over the years.

Suzuki's fascination with folk art began when he picked up one of the Shussai-gama teacups sold by *BEAMS*. It was the start of an obsession that took him to folk art stores all over Japan. In the process he got to know Keiichi Kuno, owner of the *Moyaikogei* folk art store in Kamakura, and eventually, on his own time, began to accompany Kuno on buying trips. Traveling all over Japan together they met with makers and artisans, and visited kilns. Suzuki says that Kuno seems to think of him as young successor, a bond further strengthened by Suzuki's admiration for the *Moyai kogei* building. He decided that when he built his own house, this was what it would be like.

Suzuki says that at the time, when he informed Kuno that he had decided on land to buy, his friend contacted an architect there and then. The result was the reformation, for the first time in twenty-three years, of the team that built the *Moyaikogei* building: Kuno in overall charge, joined by an architect well versed in sukiya architecture and traditional Japanese buildings, and a carpenter well-reputed in Kamakura. Suzuki himself was also actively involved in the home's design.

"I bought some graph paper, and Kuno-san and I put our heads together to design the building from the ground up. I'm also a fan of Kanjiro Kawai, so when it came to building this place, I visited Kawai's former residence in Kyoto several times. There are some parts, like the stairs, that I used for reference. But what really took my fancy was the "Chosen-bari" flooring upstairs. Chosen-bari is a construction technique devised during Korea's Joseon period by poverty-stricken common people unable to assemble sufficient boards of a uniform length or width, that involves making a wooden floor by inserting short boards between longer ones, known as "poles." I just really wanted this particular style for my house."

Here is a house where no effort has been spared to accommodate every special fancy of the owner, and three years since moving in, as the seasons come around Suzuki delights in slowly adding further touches here and there. It's a new style of Japanese house embraced by nature all year round, and by the satisfying glow of handcrafted artisanship. Out the window, the buds of the plum tree were starting to open.

鈴木 修司　*Shuji Suzuki*

1976年、三重県松阪市生れ。1998年『BEAMS』に入社。メンズ重衣料からメンズカジュアルを担当後、《fennica》の前身である《BEAMS MODERN LIVING》の店舗スタッフに。その後《fennica》のMDを経て、現在は《B:MING LIFE STORE》の生活雑貨のバイヤーとして従事。2005年、民藝の名店『もやい工藝』のオーナーである久野恵一氏との出会いにより、より深く濃く日本の伝統的な手仕事に傾倒していくことに。現在も久野氏の旅に同行し、日本各地のものづくりの現場を見て回る。ファッション、インテリア、民藝、手仕事ものが好き。また、美味しい料理とお酒をこよなく愛する。

Born 1976 in Matsuzaka, Mie. Joined *BEAMS* in 1998, working in the menswear and men's casual sections, followed by stints on the floor at *BEAMS MODERN LIVING* and in merchandising at fennica, before becoming home accessories buyer for *B:MING LIFE STORE* by BEAMS. In 2005, met the owner of *Moyai kogei*, Keiichi Kuno, and became interested in Japanese traditional handcrafts. Today, he travels with Kuno all over Jaspan visiting artisans' workshops.

http://www.bminglifestore.jp

11 / 小林 恭　小林 マナ

Takashi Kobayashi, Mana Kobayashi

Designer
Minato-ku, Tokyo

デットストックの《マリメッコ》の端切れをあわせて作ったパッチワーククロス。「柄はバラバラですけど色のトーンが
合っているので統一感がある。《マリメッコ》の生地同士は合わせやすい」とマナさん。小学生の時にいつも読んでいた
という大橋歩さんによる表紙の『生活の絵本100のアイディア』は、ヨーロッパやアメリカ、和のライフスタイルが紹介さ
れていて、今でも参考になることが多く、この本はマナさんの原点だという

上はベッド、下は収納になった寝室は2人で作った。穏やかな日差しを浴びて、猫たちが気持ち良さそうに昼寝をしていた

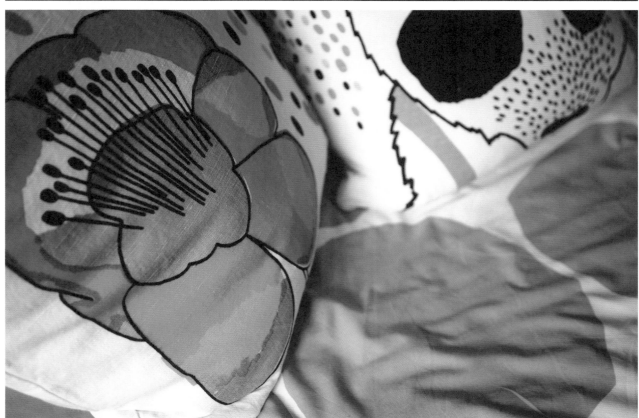

《マリメッコ》のファブリックをはじめ、色数の多い小林家で唯一ストイックな空間であるキッチン。毎日使うものだから、機能性を重視している

経年変化を楽しめる素材と
遊び心ある空間デザインを意識している

フィンランドのテキスタイルブランド、《マリメッコ》の国内外の店舗をはじめ、数多くのショップや住宅のインテリアデザインを手がける設計事務所imaの小林恭さんと小林マナさん夫妻。公私ともにパートナーの2人が愛猫たちと暮らすのは、青山と千駄ヶ谷の間にある大型の集合住宅。クリエイターやアーティストも多く住むこのヴィンテージマンションは、東京オリンピック開催の年に海外プレス関係者の宿泊施設として建てられたという。庭には大きな桜の木をはじめたくさんのグリーンが植えられている。ここに住むことを決め、スケルトンの状態から自分たちで設計した。恭さん曰く「建築を一から作る場合と同じで、もともとの部屋の条件や、窓から見える風景をきっかけに考えて、イメージを膨らませていきました」。味わいのある鉄製の窓枠などは残し、床は質感のある無垢材のフローリングに貼り替えた。「素材は本当に大切です。ある程度質感がないと空気感が良くならないので。質感のある素材で経年変化を楽しめるものがいいですね」。一方で、合板でできたキッチンの壁面には、デザインユニットenamel.が手がけたグラフィックを全面にプリントしたり、部屋のあちらこちらに猫たちが遊べる仕掛けが配されたりと遊び心も忘れない。

彼らが仕事で手がける空間デザインにも、その心意気は見て取れる。「店舗をデザインする時は、その企業やブランドイメージ、それにまつわるものなどをきっかけにして、作っていきますね。例えば《マリメッコ》のフィッティングルームには、"m"の文字を象ったフックをつけるなど、そういう細かい遊びを入れるのが好きです」と恭さん。ブランドの魅力を最大限に引き出すための空間デザインにはそのブランドに対する理解が不可欠。依頼された企業に対するリサーチもアーカイブなどを使って丹念に、徹底して行う。マナさんは、「ブランドの歴史を調べていると感動することも多くて。クライアントからよく話を聞いて、そこからデザインのポイントになる部分を探していく」のだとか。

日本の《マリメッコ》の店舗をデザインしていた2人が海外店舗を手がけるようになったのは、本国のスタッフが日本のショップを視察に来た際に彼らのデザインを気に入ってくれたから。恭さんは言う。「日本の代理店がお店を出すにあたって、日本向けに商品のラインナップを見直したんです。その際僕らもインテリアを編集し直して、きちんとものを見せたり、カテゴリーを整理したり、自分たちが思うフィンランド的なシンプルでモダンなお店を意識して作りました。その再構築の仕方が本国スタッフには新鮮だったようで、"これが《マリメッコ》の原点"と言ってもらったんです。《マリメッコ》が最も輝いていたのは1960年代。アメリカでも最も評価されていた時代でもあります。この一番《マリメッコ》らしい時代のスタイルを見直して現代に置き換えていったことが高く評価されたようです。けれどもまさか日本人の僕らに依頼がくるとは思っていなかったので驚きました。同時にもともとファンだったのでとても嬉しかったですね」

最近手がけたという海外の店舗だけ見ても、世界各地の都市とさまざまなスタイルのショップが並ぶ。ニューヨーク、ベルリン、マルメ、ヘルシンキ本社のファクトリーショップ、同じくヘルシンキのフラッグシップショップ。そして、本社にある、一般人にも開放されているカフェテリアの改装など。自然と共生し、生活に根ざしたデザインを特長とするフィンランドでは、日本人の感覚と共感することが多いことにも頷ける。恭さんは「すごく緑が多い街だから気持ち良くて。自然と触れ合って生活しているから、こういうデザインが生まれてくるというのが実感できる」。さらにマナさんも「北欧の家は窓辺がどこも美しい。以前、北欧の人たちはカーテンの柄を外に向けてつけるという話を聞いたことがあって、街を美しく飾るという理由だったと思います。窓辺を飾るという考えがとても素敵だなと思って」

フィンランド人が持つ豊かな感性とおおらかな視点を独自の視点で解釈しながら、《マリメッコ》を通して世界とつながる2人。美しく健やかな空間を生み出す、彼らの世界を舞台にした活躍はこれからも続いていく。

Consciously choosing materials that give changing pleasure as the years pass, and playful spatial design

Together, Takashi and Mana Kobayashi are the design office *IMA*, providing interior design services for a multiplicity of shops and homes, including the stores – both Japanese and other – of Finnish textile brand *Marimekko*. Partners in both work and life, the couple live with their two adored cats in a large housing complex between Aoyama and Sendagaya. The "vintage" complex, home to a sizeable contingent of creatives and artists, was built the year of the Tokyo Olympics to accommodate the foreign press. Having decided to live here, the pair gutted the apartment and redesigned it from zero. Retaining features such as the distinctive steel window frames, they pulled up the floors and replaced them with more textured, solid wood flooring. According to Takashi, "Materials truly are critical. The ambience of a place never improves without at least some texture. Textured materials, that morph in pleasing ways over the years, are the best." At the same time, there are plenty of playful touches in the home, such as graphics by the design unit *enamel.* printed all over the plywood kitchen walls, and the gadgets distributed around the rooms for feline amusement.

One can perceive that same spirit in the spatial design that is the couple's livelihood. "When we design a shop, we take the company, its brand image, associated objects etc. and use these to assemble the right look. We enjoy adding fun little touches, for example installing hooks in the shape of an "m" in the Marimekko fitting rooms." (Takashi) They also use company archives and suchlike to carry out thorough and detailed research on the commissioning client. Mana adds, "When researching the history of a brand, we're often excited by what we find. We talk a lot to the client, and seek out anything that might serve as a design feature."

Designing for the Marimekko stores in Japan, the pair ended up working on overseas stores in centers such as Helsinki and New York after staff from the company's Finnish HQ came to inspect their Japanese stores and were favorably impressed by the design. "They seem to have been struck by how we took a fresh look at the style of the 1960s, Marimekko's golden era, and transplanted that to the present day. But we were astounded. No way did we ever think they'd request a couple of Japanese for the job. At the same time, being big Marimekko fans, we were thrilled." (Takashi)

One can imagine there is much that resonates with Japanese sensibilities in Finland, where people have a symbiotic relationship with nature, and the key characteristic of design is its grounding in domestic life. Takashi says, "Towns there are very green and pleasant. You get a real sense of where this kind of design comes from when people interact so closely with the natural world." Mana adds, "Scandinavian homes are invariably attractive in the window area. I've heard that people in Scandinavia used to hang their curtains with the patterned side facing out, to brighten up the streets, I imagine. The idea of decorating the window area is highly appealing."

Informed by the rich sensibilities and easygoing outlook of the Finns, the Kobayashis connect to the world via Marimekko. Their success on the international stage, creating attractive, healthy spaces, looks set to continue for a long time yet.

小林 恭 *Takashi Kobayashi* ／ 小林 マナ *Mana Kobayashi*

1966年、兵庫県神戸市生まれ。1990年、多摩美術大学インテリアデザイン科卒業後、カザッポ＆アソシエイツに入社。（小林 恭）
1966年、東京都生まれ。1989年、武蔵野美術大学工芸デザイン科卒業。ディスプレイデザイン会社に入社。（小林 マナ）
ともに退社後、1998年、設計事務所ima（イマ）を設立。店舗設計をメインに住宅建築設計、展覧会の会場構成やプロダクトデザインなどを手がけている。2010年よりフィンランドのブランド《marimekko（マリメッコ）》の店舗も手がけ、海外にも積極的に活動の場を広げている。

Born 1966 in Hyogo. Graduated 1990 in interior design from Musashino Art University. (Takashi Kobayashi)
Born 1966 in Tokyo. Graduated 1989 in craft design from Musashino Art University. (Mana Kobayashi)
Established Design Office IMA in 1998, providing design services on projects ranging from residential architecture to exhibitions and products, but focusing mainly on store design. Since 2010, with work for Finnish textile brand *Marimekko*, their services have expanded to projects overseas.
http://www.ima-ima.com

12 /

堀内 隆志
Takashi Horiuchi

café vivement dimanche
Owner
Kamakura, Kanagawa

桜並木通りに建てられた自宅に住むようになって、桜の咲く季節が巡ってくるのが楽しみになった。何の予定もない
休日は、静かな音楽を聴きながらソファでぼんやりミサワ（愛犬）をなでているときが至福のひとときだという

自宅で一番気に入っているのは吹き抜けになった玄関。2階から螺旋階段で下りることもできる。膨大なミルコレクションは当初奥様が集めていたものだった。コーヒーと関連深いブラジルも大好きな堀内さんは、ラジオでブラジル音楽番組をもっている。ブラジルの魅力を聞くと「極端なものが共存している国。例えばアマゾンのようなジャングルから、オスカー・ニーマイヤーの建築したブラジリアのようなものまで、そのレンジの広さに惹かれる」のだとか。

"美味しいコーヒー"を絶対条件に
プラスアルファを積み重ねた店作り

『日曜日が待ち遠しい！』―フランソワ・トリュフォー監督の作品の原題が店名の由来である鎌倉の『café vivement dimanche』。カフェブームが到来した90年代当時、カフェと音楽をからめた"coffee & music"スタイルの先駆けとして注目を浴びた。人気カフェのオーナーである堀内隆志さんは、現在もお店を切り盛りしながら、コーヒーやカフェをテーマに、CDの選曲やプロデュース、ブラジル音楽のラジオ番組を担当するなど多岐にわたって活躍している。

そんな堀内さんが暮らす自宅は、鎌倉の閑静な住宅街に佇む瀟洒な一軒家。鉄製の門扉と玄関ドア、吹き抜けになった高い天井とアンティークの窓枠、洋式のバスタブなど、ヨーロッパ的な造りは以前の住人がそのまま残していったものだという。これまで何世帯かによって住み継がれ、その都度改装が繰り返されてきたことが、この家に絶妙なヴィンテージ感をもたらしている。購入の決め手になったのは「土間が広くて焙煎機が置けると思ったから」。4年前からロースター（焙煎師）を始めた堀内さんは、カフェの営業が終わって帰宅した後、自分の店と他店に卸すための豆を夜な夜な焙煎している。コーヒーについては、「嗜好品なので、感じ方は人それぞれで良い」のだとか。お店では開店以来、中深煎りと深煎りのラインナップだったが、自ら焙煎をするようになり、中煎りにも取り組むことにした。「お客さんがその日の気分で、コーヒーの味をチョイスできるようにしています。"Enjoy!"という言葉が当てはまるかわかりませんが、とにかくコーヒーを楽しんでほしいと思っています。しかめっ面で飲むより、笑顔で飲んだほうが美味しいですからね（笑）」

堀内さんが鎌倉でカフェの経営を始めたのは19年前。その道に進むことを決めたのは、アーティストの故永井宏さんとの出会いからだった。「アートはもちろん、さまざまな物事に対する考え方など、僕の人生において大きな影響を与えてくれた人」。堀内さんは大学卒業後、流通の仕事に就いたが毎日の生活に違和感を覚えていたという。「仕事に

疑問を感じる一方、楽しみといえば長期休暇でパリに行くことと、定休日に永井さんが始めた葉山の『サンライトギャラリー』に行くことでした。サンライトには、ぼくと同世代のアーティストたちが集っていて、彼らの自由な暮らし振りが本当にうらやましくて。自分の理想と現実とのギャップに苦しんでいましたね。そんな中、永井さんは『人は誰でもものづくりができる』ということを常に口にされていて、絵を描いたり立体的なものを作ったりという美術的才能に乏しかった僕は『自分だったら何ができるだろう』と真剣に考えてみたんです。そこで浮かんだのがサンライトのような風通しの良いカフェでした」

けれども当時は"喫茶店冬の時代"と呼ばれる厳しい時代。「素人だから決断できたようなもので、今のように飲食に携わっていたらカフェを始めようなんて思わなかった」。なんとか試行錯誤を繰り返しながらオープン、やがてその強い思いとこだわりは人々を惹きつけ、幅広い世代に愛される名店となっていく。「お客さんにとって、入店してから店を後にするまでの時間が"良い時間"だったと思ってもらえるように考えて店作りをしています。カフェですから、来店目的は人それぞれです。感じ方もしかり。みなさんに満足していただくのは難しいことですが、コーヒーが美味しいのは絶対条件として、プラスアルファを積み重ねていくことによって、店としての在り方を確立していっている最中です」

自宅にある膨大なミルのコレクションをはじめ、珈琲の道具に興味があるという。これまでもドリッパーセットや電動小型ミルを作ってきたが、現在は業務用のコーヒーミルを製作中だとか。「これまでカフェで培ってきた経験を生かして、後に続く人たちに何らかの手助けができたら良いなと思っています。コーヒーを淹れることや暮らしが楽しくなるようなものは、これからも作っていきたいですね」

コーヒーの香りと心地良い音楽に包まれながら、ヴィンテージ・シックな一軒家で今日もまたゆっくりと豆を挽く。家の前の歩道の桜並木が少し早めの満開を迎えていた。

First and foremost serving excellent coffee, then offering that little something extra

Café vivement dimanche takes its name from the Francois Truffaut film *Vivement dimanche!* (Confidentially Yours). Owner of the popular Kamakura cafe Takashi Horiuchi manages the cafe in a hands-on capacity while juggling myriad other ventures that include selecting and producing tracks for coffee- and cafe-themed CDs, and hosting a radio show on Brazilian music.

Horiuchi lives in a elegant house on a quiet Kamakura residential street. The European feel of the home – its iron gates and front door, soaring atrium and antique window frames, Western-style bathtub and so on – is a legacy of previous residents. Repeated alteration work by the several households that have occupied it give the house an exquisitely vintage feel. What sealed the purchase for Horiuchi was a large area of bare floor, where "it struck me I could put a coffee roasting machine."

For four years now Horiuchi has been a coffee roaster. After the cafe closes he goes home and spends night after night roasting beans for his own, and other establishments.

Horiuchi has been running a cafe for nineteen years. It was an encounter with an artist, the late Hiroshi Nagai, that set him upon his chosen course. Horiuchi explains, "He had a huge influence on my life, obviously on the way I think about art, but also about all sorts of things." After graduating from university Horiuchi got a job in logistics, but says he always felt something was not quite right about his day-to-day life. Eventually this led him to Nagai's "Sunlight Gallery" in Hayama. "Nagai-san was constantly telling us that anyone can make things, which prompted me – devoid of any artistic talent for painting pictures or making sculptures – to think seriously about what it was I could do. The answer was a cafe, a place airy and upbeat like Sunlight."

Thus followed a process of trial and error, until eventually, his determination and dedication began to attract people, and Café vivement dimanche became a well-known spot loved by all ages. According to Horiuchi, "The cafe's designed to ensure customers feel the time spent there, from the moment they enter until they leave, was quality time, time well spent. People have different reasons for coming, so it's hard to keep everyone happy, but at the moment I'm working on establishing the cafe's modus operandi by first and foremost serving excellent coffee, then offering that little something extra."

Horiuchi has an interest in coffee accessories, starting with his home collection of coffee mills, and says he is currently making coffee mills for commercial use. "Hopefully," he adds, "I can make use of the cafe experience gained thus far to in some way assist those who follow after me. Things that add fun to making coffee, to living – that's what I want to make."

Today once again this veteran cafe owner slow-roasts beans in his vintage chic house, surrounded by the aroma of coffee, and pleasant sounds. The row of blossoming cherry trees on the pavement out front were reaching their peak, just a little early.

堀内 隆志　*Takashi Horiuchi*

1967年、東京都生まれ。1994年、鎌倉で美味しいコーヒーと心地良い音楽空間を提案する『café vivement dimanche（カフェ ヴィヴモン ディモンシュ）』をスタート。現在も老若男女に愛されるカフェとして不動の人気を誇る。カフェ経営の傍ら、ブラジル音楽に精通していることから、湘南ビーチFMのブラジル音楽番組『Na Praia』を担当、「ランブリングレコーズ」ではコンピレーションCDの選曲や企画監修、プロデュース作品をリリース。ほかに音楽、カフェ、コーヒーにまつわる執筆など幅広く活躍する。近著は庄野雄治との共著『はじめてのコーヒー』（ミルブックス）。

Born 1967 in Tokyo. In 1994 opened *café vivement dimanche* offering customers good coffee and good music in Kamakura. Hosts a radio show called "Na Praia" at Shonan Beach FM and selects, organizes and plans tracks for compilation CDs. Has also produced several artists for record label *Rambling RECORDS*. Horiuchi's many endeavors also include writing about music, cafés and coffee culture, and he recently published a book with Yuji Shono titled *Hajimete no Coffee* (mille books).

http://dimanche.shop-pro.jp

13 / 青野 賢一
Kenichi Aono

BEAMS Creative Director
Meguro-ku, Tokyo

玄関に置かれた帽子のかかったコートラックは、パリのクリニャンクールのマーケットで一目惚れして購入したもの。目
的もなくふらりと出かけて買うことが多いのだとか。時代も国も意識しないから、室内には古いもの、新しいもの、アメ
リカ、北欧、ヨーロッパ、日本のものが混在している。沖縄のやちむんや小鹿田焼の皿もここでは自然となじむ

レコードや機材、楽器などが所狭しと並ぶ音楽部屋は黄色いセブンチェアがアクセントに。建築家の前川國男が
デザインした白黒のオットマンは、使い古された味わいがかえって存在感を放っていた

クラシックかつデコラティブでモダン、
どこかギリギリな感じにシンパシーを感じる

『BEAMS』でクリエイティブディレクターとして幅広く活躍する青野賢一さん。現在、ビームス創造研究所に所属し、選曲やDJ、執筆、大学、専門学校での講義など、多方面でクリエイティブな活動をしている。そんな青野さんが暮らす自宅は、天気が良い日は東京タワーが見えるというヴィンテージマンションの7階。見晴らしが良く、角部屋で窓が大きいため、リビング、寝室、楽器部屋と、どの部屋も明るい印象だ。この物件と出会ったのは運命的だったという。「レコードや機材の量が増えてきたので引っ越しを考えていましたが、条件に合う物件が全然なくて。肩を落として歩いていたら、とある古い不動産屋の窓にこの物件の情報が貼ってあって、中に入ったら『今から内見しますか?』と。そのまま見に行って……即決でした(笑)」

室内には、存在感のあるヴィンテージのL字型ソファやブルーノ・マットソンのラウンジチェア、アルネ・ヤコブセンのセブンチェア、アルヴァ・アアルトのスツールといった北欧ものや、ノーマン・チャーナーのチャーナーチェア、前川國男のオットマンなどが絶妙に配置され、インテリア好きな様子を伺わせる。「インテリアのこだわりは全然ないんです。ただ、誰でも好きなもののスタンダードみたいなものはありますよね。僕はというと、テイストやブランドをひとつのジャンルで統一するのはあまり好きじゃなくて。家には北欧もアメリカも日本のものもあるし、年代もバラバラ」というように有名か無名かは関係ないという。薔薇が描かれたインパクトのあるキャビネットは、1960年代のイギリスのヴィンテージ。「薔薇が付いている家具なんてなかなかないでしょ。そういう妙な所にぐっとくるんです。まあ、自分でもギリギリかなと思ってはいますけど(笑)。このオットマンは、前川國男さんの建築事務所の前に捨ててあったものを事務所の人にお願いしてもらってきたものです。前川さんが設計した埼玉会館のロビーで使われていたものらしいです」

青野さんが家具に興味を持つようになったのは、自社で家具を扱うようになったことが大きいという。一方で、10代の頃から観ていたヌーヴェルバーグの映画や昔の音楽や本からの影響も大きい。「以前から、当時の空間や調度品がカッコいいなっていう感覚はありました。例えば映画では、ルイ・マル監督の『鬼火』(1963年)。モーリス・ロネがパリに行く前にクローゼットから服を選ぶシーンがあるでしょう。あのシーンが最高に格好良くて。住んでいるところは施設みたいになっているけど、ああいうクラシカルな部屋の感じもいい。それから、僕の家の雰囲気とは違うんだけど、フランスの建築家ジャン・ロワイエールの展覧会図録は大切にしていて、彼のデザインやコーディネーションがすごく好きです。クラシックかつデコラティブでモダン、悪趣味ギリギリ、高級なキッチュみたいな。そんなギリギリ感が好きで、そこにすごくシンパシーを感じます。あとは、篠山紀信さんが撮影した『三島由紀夫の家』。小屋のクラシカルな雰囲気と小物の選び方、グロテスクな感じ、これもギリギリですね(笑)。『澁澤龍彦 幻想美術館』(監修・文 巖谷國士)でも、篠山紀信さんが澁澤龍彦の家を撮影しているんだけど、澁澤の家も同じような雰囲気で好きです」

ふだんから青野さんは目的を持って買い物に行くことは少ないという。家具だけでなく、レコードや本、洋服についてもふらりと出かけて偶然出会うものが多い。中でも思い入れのある一品はパリのクリニャンクールのマーケットで購入したコートラック。「一目惚れして。まだフランスの通貨がフランの時代で、値切って1,000フラン、当時日本円で3万円ぐらいだったと思います。結局、送料で10万円ほどかかりましたけど、日本のヴィンテージショップで見かけたら数倍していたので良かったという(笑)」

根底にはいつも1960年代に対する憧れのようなものがあるからか、比較的古いものが好きだという。「好きなものを選んでいくと、新しいものよりはちゃんと人の手がかけられてきたものに目が行きますね。それに人が持っているものや流行っているものにはあまり興味はなくて……。実はイームズも買ったことがない。あまのじゃくなんです(笑)」

Classic yet decorative and modern, with a penchant for the "marginal"

The home of *BEAMS* creative director Kenichi Aono is on the seventh floor of an older apartment block with a view of the Tokyo Tower on clear days. The outlook is superb, and being a corner apartment with large windows, not just the living room but every room strikes the visitor as airy and suffused with light. Inside, Aono's affinity for interiors is obvious from the perfect arrangement of a solid-looking L-shaped vintage sofa, Scandinavian pieces such as a Bruno Mathsson lounge chair and Alvar Aalto stools, a Norman Cherner chair, and ottoman by Kunio Maekawa.

Aono claims to be not at all obsessed with interiors, but does confess to a dislike for furnishing a home entirely in any single style or brand. "I've stuff here from Scandinavia, the US, Japan, all from different periods too." A striking cabinet adorned with a painting of a rose is a vintage English piece from the 1960s. "Furniture with roses on it is pretty rare. It's those odd things that grab me. Although even I'm willing to admit that tastewise, it's a bit marginal," he says with a laugh.

One of the main reasons Aono became interested in furniture, he says, is that his company started stocking it. Other major influences are the French New Wave films he first saw in his teens, and old music and books. "I'd always found the interiors and furnishings of that era cool. Take the Louis Malle film *Le feu follet* (The Fire Within; 1963). There's a scene where the main character chooses clothes from his closet before going to Paris. That has to be the most stylish movie scene ever. The classical apartment in which Maurice Ronet lives is wonderful too. As well, I have a catalog from an exhibition by French architect Jean Royère that is very precious to me, and I just love his design and coordination: classic yet modern, verging on tasteless, kind of high-class kitsch. It's that borderline quality that resonates with me. Then there's *Mishima Yukio no Ie*, photos of Yukio Mishima's house by Kishin Shinoyama. The classical feel of his mansion, the way the accessories and ornaments were chosen, the grotesqueness of it all, this too was pretty borderline (laughs). Yet another favorite of mine is Kishin Shinoyama's photos of Tatsuhiko Shibusawa's house, *Shibusawa Tatsuhiko Genso Bijutsukan*."

Aono says he rarely goes shopping with a particular objective. Generally it's a case of popping out, and happening upon something that takes his fancy. One of his best-loved objects is "a coat rack I bought at a market in Clignancourt, Paris. Love at first sight. I haggled the price down to 1,000 francs, at the time about 30,000 yen. Although in the end, with postage added it was more like 100,000," he adds with a laugh.

Aono says he prefers comparatively old things, a nod perhaps to his underlying admiration for the 1960s aesthetic. "When it comes to choosing things I like, my gaze tends to fall not so much on the new, as on what's been handled by people before. Nor am I especially interested in what others have or what's fashionable. I've never even bought an Eames, actually. Which I guess makes me a bit of a weirdo (laughs)."

青野 賢一　*Kenichi Aono*

1968年、東京都生まれ。『BEAMS』クリエイティブディレクター、《BEAMS RECORDS》ディレクター。プレス職などを経て、現在はビームス創造研究所に所属し、執筆、展示やイベントの企画運営、大学、専門学校での講義など、主に社外の仕事を行う。DJ、選曲家としても知られ、山崎真央（gm projects）、鶴谷聡平（NEWPORT）との選曲ユニット「真っ青」としても活動中。著書に『迷宮行き』（BCCKS／天然文庫）がある。

Born 1968, raised in Tokyo. Creative Director, *BEAMS*. Director, *BEAMS RECORDS*. After working in advertising and promotion, joined *BEAMS Creative Reasearch Department*, engaging in music selection, DJing, writing, and other activities mainly outside of the company. Member of the music-selection unit *Massao*. Author of *Meikyu-yuki* (Mystery bound; BCCKS/Tennen Bunko).

http://www.beams.co.jp

14 / ルーカス・B.B.

Lucas Badtke-Berkow

Knee High Media Japan CEO / Creative Director
Shibuya-ku, Tokyo

朝のキッチンには美しい光が燦々と差し込む。一年を通して季節を感じることができる2階は、毎日スタッフと共有するパブリックスペース

銭湯に行くのも楽しみのひとつ。仕事の区切りに木の桶のお風呂セットを持ってふらっと行くことが、いい息抜きになっている

都会の喧騒から離れた住宅街に佇む日本家屋は、和風と洋風をミックスしたようなモダンな造りが魅力。築70年を超すが、改装は床と壁だけ、構造自体はほぼそのままで使用している。プライベートスペースの1階には、アメリカ、オーストラリア、インド、日本など、旅先で偶然出会って持ち帰ったアイテムがディスプレイされており、無国籍な中にゆるやかな調和が感じられる。縁側から見渡せる四季折々のグリーンが目にも鮮やか。植栽も和洋折衷で個性的だ

心を開き、複眼的な思考を持つことが
仕事と生活に新たなアイデアをもたらす

「朝の時間に来てもらえる？ キッチンにいい光が入るから——」。オファーにそう答えてくれたのは、ユニークな視点と独自の切り口で、日本を拠点にさまざまなクリエイティブ活動を行う、ニーハイメディア・ジャパンCEO兼クリエイティブディレクターのルーカス・バテキ・バルコさん。仕事場と住居が一緒になったルーカスさんのお宅は、渋谷の静かな住宅街に佇む、木造2階建ての一軒家。築70年、風情のある日本家屋は、ゆるやかな坂道に沿って建てられており、2階が玄関になったモダンな構造だ。上段のフロアには、キッチンとダイニング、段差で区切られた事務所スペースがあり、スタッフのデスクが並ぶ。階下は、壁を取り払った、広々とした空間のプライベートルーム。縁側から、柿の木や紅葉、ブルーベリー、葉牡丹など、植栽に彩られた庭と小さな池が見渡せる。

「目覚めとともに朝日がたっぷり入る、この日本家屋が好きなんだ。この家を作った人が、都会と自然の良さをうまく取り込めるように考えたんだと思う。古い日本家屋の物件は少ないから、こういった生活ができるのはかなり貴重だよね」。とはいえ、インテリアが和風一辺倒にならないのもルーカスさんならでは。部屋の中には、国内外の旅先で手に入れたというものたちが随所にディスプレイされていて、セレクトや色使いなど、無国籍な感覚やセンスが目を引く。「旅で買い物をする時に、今あるものたちとどうやって組み合わせようかと考えるのが好きなんだ。家に置くなら、ちょっとでもハッピーになれるものがいい。そういったものたちが少しずつ増えていくと、毎日の生活も楽しくなるからね。ここにはオーストラリアのブーメラン、島根の民芸、インドの神様のオブジェ、青森で買った座布団……テイストはバラバラだけど、偶然出会って持ち帰ったものが一つ一つの旅の思い出になっている。自分にしかわからないけど、眺めたり、使ったりするたびにストーリーが見えてきて、そういうのが楽しい」

この家で暮らし始めてからライフスタイルも変化した。以前、事務所として使用していた時は仕事も人も多くなり過ぎてしまい、心身ともに疲れてしまったことがあったという。そんな理由から、今は会社をコンパクトにして、プライベートと仕事場を一緒にすることにした。

「スタッフとは、常に家族みたいな距離で仕事をしたいと思っている。だから、ここでご飯を一緒に食べるし、打ち合わせもする。この空間をみんなで共有することで、すごく居心地が良くなったんだ。そもそもぼくらが手がけるクリエイティブは、マーケティングによるものではなく作り手のテンションの問題。面白い人やもの、場所を紹介していくことで、誰かの人生がインスパイアされるかもしれない。いいものをみんなでシェアしたいという気持ちで作っている。ぼくたちの"気"が入ってないと、そのまま作ったものに現れてしまうからね」

これまで、サブカルチャーに始まり、旅、子供、植物、アウトドアなどをテーマにした雑誌やイベントを数多く手がけてきた。世の中が注目するタイミングよりいつも半歩先を行く。その嗅覚を磨くためには「常に外に向かって開いている状態でいること」が大切だという。「人との会話から影響を受けることが多いから、誰に対しても偏見を持たないようにしている。そうやって心を開いていると自然と面白いアイデアや発想が入ってくるんだ。あとは、『TOKION』を作っていた頃から"wide screen（ワイドスクリーン）"という言葉を使っているんだけど、世界をいろんな角度で見ていくことがとても大切だと思っている。生活でも仕事でもそのバランス感覚を大事にしているよ」

この古い日本家屋での暮らしからも新たな発見を得ることができるという。「庭に柿の木があるんだけど、たくさん実った年は、友達に"おすそわけ"の気持ちで贈る。そういう日本の習慣一つとっても、この家で毎日を過ごすことで、昔の人の暮らしぶりが何となくわかるんだ。だから、日本の良い文化をメディアで伝えることはもちろん、自分の生活を通して伝えていければと思っているよ」

Opening the mind to multiple ways of thinking engenders new ideas for work and living

"Could you come in the morning? The light in the kitchen is really good then..."

Thus Lucas Badtke-Berkow, CEO and Creative Director of *Knee High Media Japan*, kindly agreed to our interview. Badtke-Berkow's combined home and workplace is a two-storey wooden house nestled in a quiet Shibuya neighborhood. The character-filled 70-year-old Japanese-style home, built on a gentle slope, is modern in configuration, with its entrance hall on the second floor. Also on this top floor are the kitchen, dining area and office space. Downstairs is devoted to a spacious private room. From the porch are views of a colorful ornamental garden and small pond.

Badtke-Berkow says he loves the way this Japanese-style home fills with sunlight as he wakes up in the morning. Dotted throughout the house are items picked up on his travels in Japan and abroad, mementos notable for the absence of any distinctive national style or aesthetic in their color or choosing. If a thing is going to be in his house, he notes, it might as well be something that adds a little joy to the place. "If you keep slowly accumulating things of this sort, day-to-day living just becomes more fun."

Badtke-Berkow's lifestyle has also changed since he started living in the house. Before combing his living and working space, he says, there was too much work and too many people, exhausting him both physically and mentally. Then in a step towards Japan's past he decided to downsize the company, and combine workplace and private space.

"Ideally I prefer to work alongside my staff like family, so we eat together here, and hold discussions. Sharing this space among us is just so much more pleasant. The kind of work we do doesn't come down to marketing, but creative tension. By showcasing an interesting person or object or place, we may help someone feel more inspired in their own life. Our desire is to share good things with others. If we don't inject our own spirit into things, it soon shows in what we produce."

Armed with a unique perspective and unconventional approach, Badtke-Berkow stays a half-step ahead of the trends. To hone this talent for sniffing out the latest thing, he says it is vital to "be constantly open and looking outward."

"I'm often influenced by conversations with people, so I try not to harbor prejudices about anyone. If your heart and mind are open, interesting ideas and concepts will naturally come in. Since *TOKION* I've been using the term 'wide screen,' and 'organic' to describe our editing style. In my view it's critical to keep looking at the world from a variety of angles. Maintaining that balance is important to me."

Living in this old Japanese house is in itself a source of new discoveries. "There's a persimmon tree in the garden, and in years when it fruits I distribute the persimmons to friends, in the Japanese tradition of 'osusowake.' That single old custom is an example of how, spending every day in this house, you start to get some idea how people once lived. So hopefully I can show what's good about Japanese culture not only through the media I created, but also through my own lifestyle."

ルーカス・B.B. *Lucas Badtke-Berkow*

1971年、アメリカ・ボルティモア生まれ。サンフランシスコ育ち。1993年に来日、1996年にニーハイメディア・ジャパンを設立し、カルチャー誌『TOKION』を出版。その後もトラベルライフスタイル誌『PAPERSKY』やキッズ誌『mammoth』を手がけながら、『Metro min.』(スターツ出版)や『Planted』(毎日新聞社)など、数多くのメディアに関わる。ファミリー向け野外フェスティバル「マンモス・パウワウ」や日本各地を自転車で巡る「ツール・ド・ニッポン」のイベント企画やプロデュースなど、雑誌以外のさまざまなフィールドでもクリエイティブ活動を行う。

Born 1971 in Baltimore, raised in San Francisco. Came to Japan in 1993, and in 1996 established *Knee High Media Japan*, publishing the culture magazine *TOKION*, followed by travel/lifestyle magazine *PAPERSKY* and kids magazine *MAMMOTH*. Has worked as editor-in-chief and creative director on various media including *Metro min.* (Starts Publishing) and *Planted* (The Mainichi Newspapers), and has since expanded his creative practice beyond print media to organizing and producing events. such as mammoth pow-wow and the PAPERSKY Tour de Nippon.

http://www.khmj.com

15 / 江口 宏志　山本 祐布子

Hiroshi Eguchi, Yuko Yamamoto

Bookshop Owner, Illustrator
Setagaya-ku, Tokyo

仕事と子育てをこなす山本さんは、忙しい毎日でも「何か出したらすぐに片付ける」という習慣を心がけている。
それが常にクリーンな空間をキープする秘訣なのだとか。最近ベッドルームの壁に知り合いの作品を飾った。
「それが楽しくて。これからもっと"飾ること"がしたい」

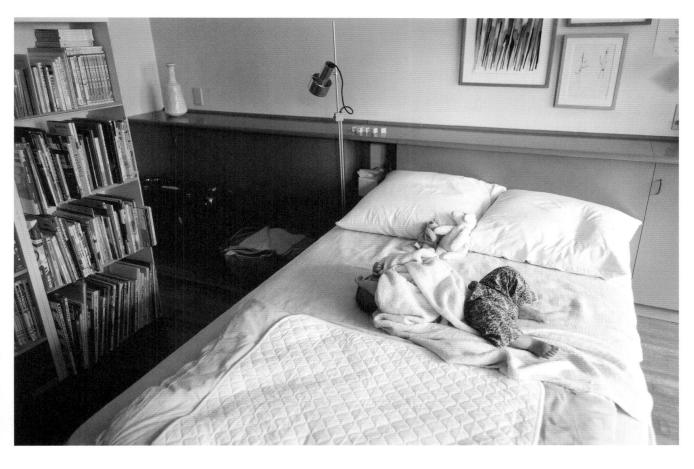

山本さんの作業スペースは自然光が差し込む清々しい空間。一方、江口さんのお気に入りのスペースである書庫は、世界各国のペーパーバックやヴィジュアルブックのコレクションが圧巻。膨大な蔵書に埋もれて、ここで作業をすることもあるという。「僕は彼女と違って、いろんなことを取り散らかしてやるのが合っているんです」

気に入ったものがなければ作る、
妥協のないもの選びが気持ちの良い空間を生む

東京・青山にあるブックショップ『UTRECHT』のオーナー江口宏志さんと、イラストを中心に、切り絵やドローイングなどを手がけるクリエイターの山本祐布子さん夫妻は、閑静な住宅街に佇むテラスハウスに愛娘ミトちゃんと3人で暮らしている。「キッチンの床のタイルと一部ペンキを塗った以外は手を加えていない」という自宅は、海外暮らしが長かったオーナーが帰国後に建てた家というだけあって、どこかモダンで洋風な造り。落ち着いたトーンの白い壁と、グレーに塗られた扉や窓枠の組み合わせが独特のセンスの良さを醸し出している。

山本さんは、女性を中心に幅広い層から支持されている人気作家。リビングスペースの一角にアトリエがあり、庭に向かって大きく開かれた窓からは柔らかな陽の光と心地良い風が入る。毎日この場所で仕事と子育てをこなしているとは思えないほど、クリーンで落ち着きのある空間が広がっている。「こまめに整えるようにしています。仕事や作業が終わったら整えるということはいつも意識していますね。自分の気持ちも整理ができるんです」。もの選びの視点も極めてシンプルで感覚的。「自分が好きかだけでなく、常にその空間の雰囲気に似合うものだけを探して選んでいます」。だが、セレクトに妥協はない。バスルームにかけられたシャワーカーテンは、良いものが見つからなかったという理由から、山本さんが自作をした。残った布でミトちゃんのワンピースをお揃いで仕立てたという微笑ましいエピソードも。

江口さんも「例えば"ベビー用品"はとにかく種類が多い。情報に踊らされることなく、本当に必要なものかどうか買う前に一度考えますね」。常に客観的に判断して慎重にセレクトしているから、必要以上にものが増えることはない。けれども、だからこそ一つ一つのものとの出会いやストーリーは大切にしているという。「作り手の顔が見えるものが好きなんです。そういう意味で友達から買うことが多いですね。気に入ったものが見つからなくて、プロダクトデザイナーの白鳥浩子さんと一緒に椅子を作ったり、2人組の陶器作家、

崔聡子さんと蔵原智子さんに器を作ってもらったり……。それから、使えるアート作品が定期的に届く、"The Thing Quarterly"というアメリカの頒布会で手に入れた陶器もあります。できるだけルーツが面白いとか、作っている人が面白いといった作品を選びますね」。その一方で、現在はものを買うという行為に対して興味をなくしつつあるとも。「ものを通じて作り手と知り合って、そこから何かを始めることが好きなんです。実際にあまり買い物はしていません。本以外は(笑)」

本という"もの"だけは接し方が少し違うと笑う江口さんは、自宅の庭の奥に、幅6m、奥行80cmほどの専用の書庫を持っている。中は足を踏み入れるのがやっと、床から天井まで膨大な量の本がぎっしりと収納されている。江口さんにとっては、愛おしい本たちに囲まれた隠れ家のような空間だ。この中から暮らしにまつわる本を聞いてみると、おすすめの海外書籍を紹介してくれた。まず、アイルランド出身の建築家兼イラストレーターが家のまわりの自然を描いた『IN THE WILDS』(Nigel Peake)は独特の視点が素敵な本。『Usefulness in Small Things』(Kim Colin & Sam Hecht)は、5ポンド以下の、単機能だけど有能なものばかりを集めた写真集。"家にある100個のもの"というテーマで描かれた『100 Things in My Room』(Misato Ban)はユトレヒトで作った本。さらに、ナタリー・ドゥ・パスクエのドローイングでものの配置の妙を解く『Arranging Things : A Rhetoric of Object Placement』(Leonard Koren)や、糸で仕切った独特の空間構成が秀逸な作品集『Fred Sandback』(Fred Sandback)、キュレーターでアートコレクターの自宅を紹介している『A way of life』(Kettle's Yard)の全6冊。

これらの書籍には、毎日の暮らしを楽しむためのアイデアや、気持ちの良い空間を生み出すためのヒントが満載で、夫妻も参考にしているという。鮮やかなグリーンが広がる庭を眺めながら「これから庭に埋めた種の成長と子供の成長を一緒に見守っていくのが楽しみです」と笑う2人。家族で過ごすかけがえのない空間は、ぬくもりと優しさに満ちていた。

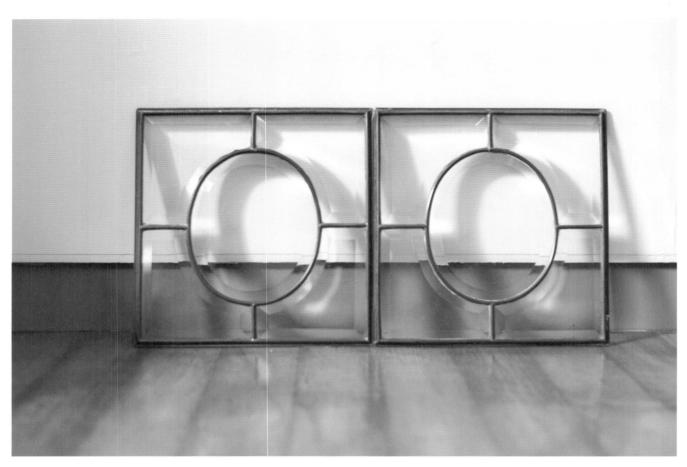

If nothing on offer takes your fancy, make one yourself:
an uncompromising approach to interior selections that begets truly feelgood spaces

Hiroshi Eguchi, owner of *UTRECHT*, a bookshop in Aoyama, Tokyo, and Yuko Yamamoto, a creator of papercut art, drawings etc., live with their baby girl Mito in a terrace house in a quiet residential neighborhood. The house, which leans toward the Modernist and Western in construction, is testament to the couple's excellent style sense, thanks to its combination of understated white walls and gray-painted doors and window frames.

Yamamoto's studio occupies a corner of the living room. Mellow sunlight and a pleasant breeze enter through windows opening wide out onto the garden. The space is so neat and uncluttered it's hard to believe she works and takes care of a child here every day. "I'm always mindful of keeping things very tidy," she says. "It helps keep my own mind in order, too." Yamamoto's approach to choosing items for the house also tends toward the very simple and sensory, and she says she only picks objects that complement the ambience of any particular space. Nor does she ever compromise on her selections. The shower curtain hanging in the bathroom is one she made herself, having failed to find a good one anywhere. And rather delightfully, she used the leftover fabric to run up a dress for little Mito.

Eguchi is equally cautious in his choices, and avoids acquiring any more "stuff" than necessary. What he does value are encounters with things, and the stories behind them.

"I like to be able to see the maker's face in a thing. For that reason we buy a lot from friends. Making a chair with product designer Hiroko Shiratori, having ceramic artist team Satoko Sai and Tomoko Kurahara make containers for us, for example... We also have ceramics obtained from American mail order project 'The Thing Quarterly'

which delivers usable artworks on a periodic basis. Where possible I go for objects with interesting origins, or made by an interesting person."

At the bottom of the garden Eguchi has a storeroom measuring about six meters wide and 80cm deep, devoted entirely to books. Crammed with a vast collection stretching from floor to ceiling, it barely has standing room. For Eguchi this is a secret hideaway of sorts, a place to surround himself in his favorite reading. When asked to pick some books on living and lifestyle from this collection, he first of all recommended *In the Wilds* by Nigel Peake, in which the Irish architect and illustrator depicts the natural world around his house. He also suggested *Usefulness in Small Things* (Kim Colin & Sam Hecht), a collection of items with just a single function, but all quite ingenious, and all costing under five pounds; *100 things in my room* (Misato Ban) depicting 100 objects in the author's house; and *Arranging Things: A Rhetoric of Object Placement* (Leonard Koren), which demystifies the art of arranging objects, with drawings by Nathalie Du Pasquier. *Fred Sandback* (Fred Sandback) a collection of photos outstanding for its unconventional approach to spatial configuration, and *A Way of Life* (Kettle's Yard), showcasing the home of a curator and art collector, completed a total of six books.

Crammed with ideas for getting more enjoyment out of everyday living, and hints for creating feel-good spaces, Eguchi says the couple also use these books for reference. Gazing out at the vivid greens of the garden, the smiling pair intimate that they look forward to watching the seeds they've planted there grow alongside their daughter. In this home, a space indispensable to family living brimmed with warmth and congeniality.

江口 宏志 *Hiroshi Eguchi*

1972年生まれ。アーティストブックの出版、国内外のインディペンデントパブリッシャーなど、本を用いた活動を行う複合的なブックショップ『UTRECHT（ユトレヒト）』代表。アジア最大のブックフェア「THE TOKYO ART BOOK FAIR」を企画・運営するZINE'S MATE共同ディレクターを務める。

Born 1972. President of the multiplex bookstore/book-related lifestyle shop and publishers of artist books UTRECHT NOW IDeA. Co-director of ZINE'S MATE, organizers and operators of the Tokyo Art Book Fair, Asia's largest book fair.

山本 祐布子 *Yuko Yamamoto*

1977年生まれ。京都精華大学デザイン学科卒業。切り絵、ドローイングを用いた雑誌や広告のイラストレーションのほか、プロダクトデザインなど幅広く手がける。

Born 1977, raised in Tokyo. Graduated in textile design from Kyoto Seika University. In addition to illustrations incorporating papercut art and drawings for magazines and advertising, she engages in product design and a wide range of creative endeavors.

http://utrecht.jp http://www.nowidea.info http://zinesmate.org http://yukoyamamoto.jp

16 / 柚木 沙弥郎
Samiro Yunoki

Fabric-Dyeing Artist
Shibuya-ku, Tokyo

売り物や道端に落ちているものなど、すべて柚木さんの琴線に触れたものたちが棚いっぱいに並ぶ。
中でも素朴なフォークアートは見ているだけで楽しい気持ちになるのだとか

アンティークのタイルはポルトガル（上）とグアテマラ（下）のもの。それぞれ旅先で買ってきた。
「何の接点もないけど一緒に置くとしっくりくる」

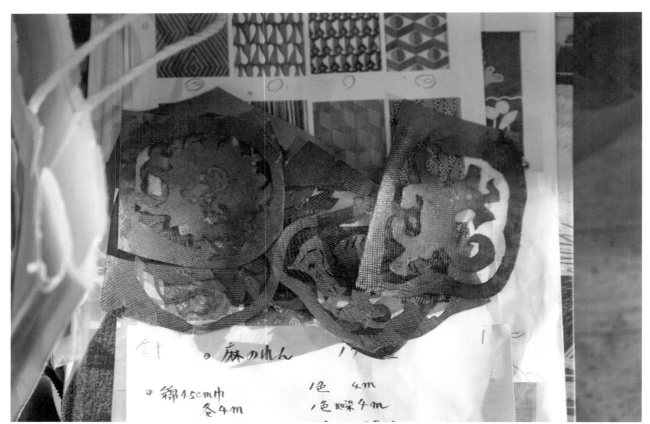

制作はどこでもやるからいつも道具を持って歩いているという。型紙やスケッチ、思いつきのメモ、そして作品
までもが部屋のいたるところに置かれていた

フォークアートを見て悟った
「ものっていうのは、嬉しくなくちゃつまらない」

　今年91歳を迎えた柚木沙弥郎さんは、人間国宝の染色工芸家、芹沢銈介に師事した現役の染色家であり、アーティストだ。時に大胆、時に繊細、さまざまな表情を持つ作品群は、色やモチーフも自由でユニーク。どれも力強く、生命力に溢れている。そんな柚木さんが制作をする場所は、アトリエとプライベートを兼ねた3階建ての落ち着いた佇まいの一軒家。渋谷区の閑静な住宅街の一角、ショッピングが好きな柚木さんは、この場所がお気に入りで昭和25年から住み続けている。

　昭和後期に建て替えたという自宅はモダンでシンプルな外装。だが、一歩足を踏み入れると、そこは巨大なおもちゃ箱のような空間が広がる。室内には世界各国の民芸品や郷土玩具、オブジェやおもちゃたちが、棚から梁といった部分にまで、所狭しと飾ってある。「旅先でよく買ったよ。ここにはメキシコ、インド、エチオピア、北欧やアメリカ……いろいろな国のものが集まっている。でも集めようと思ったことはいっぺんもないんだ。向こうから目に飛び込んでくるんだから仕方ないよ(笑)」

　師匠芹沢の勧めもあって、初めて海外を訪れたのは45歳の時。エジプト、トルコ、ギリシャを皮切りに、アフリカ、アメリカ、アジア、北欧、中南米と旅をしてきた中で、さまざまなものに触れてきた。一方で、部屋の中には古びたボールや錆びたペンチの姿も。近所や公園を散歩している時でも心に留まったものは「つい拾ってしまう」のだとか。好奇心のおもむくままに集めているようでいて、琴線に触れるのは共通している。「とにかく面白いと思うもの、ワクワクするもの。お店の人に『こういうものがあります』って見せられたものよりも、自分で見て、一番最初に目に入ったものがいいんだ。すべては直感だよ。ここにあるものは全部そう。昔、民藝運動を提唱した柳宗悦さんや陶芸家の濱田庄司さん、芹沢先生はしきりに『これは感じがあるね』と言っていた。ものに生き生きとした個性があって、こちらに訴えかけてくるかどうか、感じるかどうかが大切なんだ」

　アメリカ・ニューメキシコ州にあるインターナショナル・フォーク・アート・ミュージアムのアレキサンダー・ジラルドのコレクションや香川県にある猪熊弦一郎の美術館MIMOCAを見て共感することも多く、中でも特にプリミティブなものに心惹かれるという。「メキシコやペルーの土細工みたいな素朴なものが好きだね。古代の人と今の人と少しも変わらないものがあるんだ。よくこんなものを作るなぁと感心する。楽しいものを作ることができる人たちは素晴らしい。こういう作品を見た時に、ぼくは『ものっていうのは、嬉しくなくちゃつまらない』って悟ったんだ」。柚木さんは、キャリアのスタートこそ染色だったが、今ではジャンルにとらわれることなく、版画やガラス絵、絵本などの平面作品から人形などの立体作品まで幅広く手がけている。その自由な創作活動には、温かみやユーモアのある素朴なフォークアートが影響を与えている。

　2008年には初めてパリで個展を開催。2010年まで3年連続開催を果たした。モダンで斬新な作風に、現地の人々も80代のアーティストと聞いて驚いていたという。「いろんな人が見に来てくれたよ。でもフランスでは、まず『今作ったものはどれだ?』と聞かれる。これまでどんなことをやってきたとか、ましてや学歴や職歴とか、過去のことは一切関係ない。『今あなたは何をやっている? 何に興味がある?』そういう考え方なんだ」。長年にわたり創作を続けてきた柚木さんもまた、「今どういうことに生きているかが大切」と断言する。その上で毎日を豊かに生きるための秘訣を教えてくれた。

　「人間はいつもワクワクしていないとダメなんだ。老若男女関係なく、何かに憧れを抱いたり、楽しいと思ったり、そういうものを常に求めていればいいんじゃないかな。対象は何だっていい。肝心なものは情熱だよ。あとは気力。老人になれば何でも忘れてしまうし、悲観しても記憶力は追いつきっこない。そんなことより、情熱を持って白紙で立ち向かえばいいんだ。ワッショ、ワッショってね(笑)」

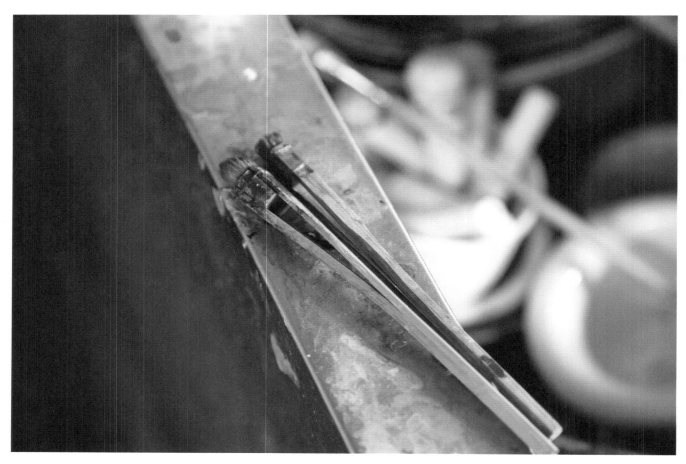

Folk art led to a realization that things must be fun, or what's the point?

Samiro Yunoki, who turned ninety-one this year, is a fabric-dyeing artist of Living National Treasure status, a working dyer who studied under Keisuke Serizawa, and an artist. His works in all their myriad manifestations – at times bold, at others subtle and delicate – are truly unique in their freestyle approach to coloring and motifs, and without exception powerful and dynamic. The creator of this remarkable oeuvre works in a nondescript three-storey house that also serves as his home. Though modern and simple outside, once inside the house is revealed as a giant toybox, crammed from shelves to rafters with folk art and traditional toys from around the world, art objects and children's playthings.

Yunoki made his first overseas trip at the age of forty-five, partly at the urging of his mentor Serizawa. Traveling in Africa, the United States, Asia, Scandinavia and Latin America has brought him into contact with a multiplicity of objects. He appears to collect whatever excites his curiosity, the common factor being that all tug at the heartstrings in some way. "First and foremost a thing has to be interesting, get the heart racing. The first thing to catch the eye is the best. It's all down to intuition. Does an object have its own distinct, dynamic personality; is it appealing in some way, does it evoke some kind of feeling? This is what's important."

Yunoki says that the likes of the Alexander Girard collection at the International Folk Art Museum in New Mexico, and MIMOCA, the Genichiro Inokuma museum in Kagawa, tend to resonate with him, particularly the more primitive pieces. "I prefer more simple, rustic things like the claywork of places like Mexico and Peru. In many ways people today are no different to our distant ancestors. People who can make fun things are wonderful. When I saw pieces like this I realized that if a thing is not fun, what's the point?"

Yunoki may have started his career in dyeing, but these days his interests have diversified across genres, from two-dimensional disciplines such as printmaking, glass painting and picturebooks, to dolls and other objects. This flexible approach to creative practice is influenced by the simplicity of folk art with its warmth and humor.

In 2008 Yunoki staged his first solo exhibition in Paris, going on to do so for three years in a row to 2010. Apparently the locals were amazed to find such modern, unconventional work to be the product of an artist in his eighties.

"All kinds of people came for a look," he says. "But in France, the first thing people want to know is, which is your latest work. What you've being doing up to then is irrelevant. That's how they think there."

Having pursued a creative career for so many years now, Yunoki is adamant that, "The important thing is what you're living for now." Accordingly he told us his secret to making the most of every day.

"Human beings constantly need something to inspire and excite them. Young or old, we should keep seeking out that which we enjoy, things we aspire to, whatever those may be. The key is to have something you're passionate about. And willpower. When you're old you forget everything. There's no point being down about it: your memory just can't keep up. Instead I think it's better to put yourself in front of a blank page, equipped with that passion and enthusiasm. As in, just keep getting up and at 'em (laughs)."

柚木 沙弥郎 *Samiro Yunoki*

1922年、東京都生まれ。柳宗悦が提唱する「民藝」との出会いを機に、芹沢銈介の型染めカレンダーに魅せられ弟子入り、染色の道を志す。50年以上にわたる制作活動の一方で、1972年、女子美術大学の教授に就任、87年に学長に就任し、91年、退職。2008年〜2010年、パリの『GALERIE L'EUROPE』で、3年連続で個展を開催し、現地で高い評価を得る。2012年4月、神奈川県立近代美術館『村山亜土作「夜の絵」』とともに 柚木沙弥郎展2012』、2013年5月、東京の世田谷美術館『いのちの旗じるし』が好評を博す。現在も現役の作家として精力的に創作に励む。

Born 1922 in Tokyo. Smitten by a stencil-dyed calendar by Keisuke Serizawa, went to study under the master in pursuit of a career as a fabric-dyeing artist. Has since been creating artworks for over fifty years that have been shown in numerous solo and group exhibitions. Held solo exhibitions at Galerie L'Europe in Paris for three consecutive year from 2008 to 2010, and his solo show at Museum of Modern Art, Kamakura in 2012 also won critical acclaim. He continues to produce inspiring new works, a body of which was on view at his 2013 solo show "The Emblem of Life" at Setagaya Art Museum, Tokyo.

http://www.samiro.net

LIFECYCLING

イデーが訪ねる、眺めのいい住処

The Story of 16 Inspiring Homes

2013年10月7日　初版第1刷発行
2014年 7月8日　　第2刷発行

Photographers

牧野吉宏　*Yoshihiro Makino P.003–059*

平野太呂　*Taro Hirano P.062–073*

関 めぐみ　*Megumi Seki P.074–083, P.142–153*

三部正博　*Masahiro Sanbe P.084–095, P.108–119, P.132–141, P.154–165*

高木康行　*Yasuyuki Takaki P.096–107*

今津聡子　*Satoko Imazu P.120–131*

木寺紀雄　*Norio Kidera P.166–175, P.188–199*

間瀬 修　*Osamu Mase P.176–187*

Director & Editor
柴田隆寛　*Takahiro Shibata (EATer)*

Editor & Writer
熱田千鶴　*Chizuru Atsuta (EATer)*

Coordinator & Writer [LA]
武藤 彩　*Aya Muto*

Book Designer
竹田麻衣子　*Maiko Takeda (Lim)*

English Translation [TOKYO]
パメラ・ミキ・アソシエイツ　*Pamela Miki Associates*

Managing Editors
及川さえ子　*Saeko Oikawa (PIE BOOKS)*
吉村真樹　*Maki Yoshimura (PIE BOOKS)*

Planning & Supervisor
大島忠智　*Tadatomo Oshima (IDÉE)*

発行人　三芳寛要
発行元　株式会社パイ インターナショナル
〒170-0005 東京都豊島区南大塚2-32-4　TEL: 03-3944-3981　FAX: 03-5395-4830　sales@pie.co.jp

制作協力　PIE BOOKS
印刷・製本　図書印刷株式会社